Touring on Two Wheels

Touring on Two Wheels

The Bicycle Traveler's Handbook

Dennis Coello

Nick Lyons Books

For Dave

Printed in the United States of America

10   9   8   7   6   5   4   3   2   1

Library of Congress Cataloging-in-Publication Data

Coello, Dennis.
    Touring on two wheels.

    Includes index.
    1. Bicycle touring.   I. Title.
GV1044.C64   1988   796.6   88-2750
ISBN 0-941130-79-7 (pbk.)

Line illustrations by Kris Peterson.

Contents

Acknowledgements

Most of my touring is solo, but book production is a *group* endeavor. I therefore wish to extend my heartfelt thanks to: Kris Peterson, for her excellent artwork; David Taff, for the "Grade Comparison" drawing; Gary Topping and Linda Prosperie, for their darkroom assistance; Brian Thurgood (who took a great deal of time away from his mountain bike touring company "The Road Less Traveled"), Willa Huelskamp, and Tara Curry, for photo production; the staffs of two Salt Lake bike shops—Bicycle Center (Philip Blomquist, Brad Hansen, Wayne Baxter, Ken Gronseth, Kenneth Acklin, Scott Tanner), and Stout Bicycles (Willa Huelskamp, Barry Makarewicz, Bob Stout, John West), for supplying equipment, modeling, and answering many questions; Rosemary Vickers, for workspace; the staff of Borge Andersen Photo Lab (Charlotte Stewart, Ann Asper, Jan Schou), for general lab assistance and personal support; my editor, Peter Burford; and the many unnamed individuals who appear in the photos and paragraphs of this book.

Finally, I wish simply to say hello once more to the thousands of people I've met around the world during my quarter century of cycle touring. For the smiles, waves, road directions, food, water, places to sleep, and companionship—thanks.

Introduction

I BET I KNOW what went through your mind when you saw the title: "Oh, Lord. Another book on cycle touring."

I don't blame you. In fact, I had the same response when first contacted by the publishers. Not wishing to offend, and hoping to interest them in one or two of the manuscripts collecting dust in my files, I thanked them for thinking of me, graciously declined, and asked if they would be interested in five hundred pages on cycling the Lewis and Clark Trail.

"Uh, let's talk about that project later" was the reply, one that I had anticipated. But what surprised me was what followed.

"Look," they argued, "we know there are a few how-to books on touring. We've read them. A lot of facts, a great deal of detail, written by someone who's done it a few times over a few years. But from what we can gather you've toured for more than *twenty* years, and this is *all* you do."

I waited for the partially suppressed laughter, or the so-when-will-you-grow-up line most often delivered by a somber-faced relative or close friend. It didn't come.

"What we want," the publishers continued, "is not just *how* to tour, but *why*.

That gave me pause. They weren't asking for the simple nuts-and-bolts approach, the kind of book that reads like a string of bike magazine articles. All that information would of course be included—which kind of bike for particular rides, best equipment for the tour, training, planning, repairs, and more. But for once I was being asked to write as I feel, that these are but the techniques of touring, not the substance.

Most books on biking, and almost all magazines, are devoted to technique. Written by (and seemingly for) MIT graduates, they endlessly discuss the bicycle's tube angles and frame composition. When they do get around to the rider it is to treat him like a gerbil on an exercise wheel, to probe, analyze, disassemble. Can he operate more efficiently if dressed in lycra, equipped with cleats, taught to keep his fats low and RPM high? And what if we teardrop his helmet and make sleek his water bottle; will it increase *speed*?

Efficiency is for racers. It is also for the rest of us during our work week, and to a humane extent important to us when we ride. That is, I prefer light bikes to heavy ones, eighteen speeds to three, toeclips and straps rather than the energy-wasting pedals of my yesteryears. But if I dress up in skin-tight, lizard-bright lycra and Italian racing shoes I'll never get to know the locals in some small-town café. It's a simple matter of human nature: look as if you're from another world and you'll be treated that way.

That doesn't mean I trade in my ball cap for a sombrero when riding through Arizona, or clamp aboard my head a "John Deere" cap when cycling in Missouri. What it does mean is that by dressing somewhat normally, and by taking my time in traveling the countryside, I get across the message that *I* am not the focus of my ride. Watch a racer's furtive glances as he speeds through town, or a loud touring group as they rush through a meal while pouring over topo maps. *They* are the experience, not their surroundings.

If speed is the goal, if efficiency is all, if the self-contained group is sufficient company, that's perfect. The only thing you lose is everything else.

Countless times over the past twenty-plus years of touring I've had bib-overalled farmers invite me to their tables, I've listened to steelworkers discuss a strike, attended town meetings, been invited to buck hay, shear sheep, lay irrigation pipe, eat dinner, spend the night, and asked to write, to come again. I've heard tales of the Depression, of war, of business success, of losing one's first-born, of local history, and more happiness and human woe than that told to shrinks and bartenders.

Why should a stranger, pedaling into town, become privy to such privacies and be trusted in the home? Part of it, no doubt, is the mode of travel. Who can have harm on his mind if his mode of escape is two unmotorized wheels? But a larger part, I'm sure, is that played by the position in which the bicycle places the biker. People feel at ease asking cyclists how far they've come, where they're headed, what kind of distance they can do in a day and why in the world they are doing it. The biker can respond with monosyllables, thinking all the while

Right: The Cyclist Magazine *staff crosses the San Juan River in southern Utah—on an off-road (and sometimes "on-bridge") mountain bike tour.*

that he's already answered the same questions six times that day. Or he can take the opportunity to reply, then turn the questions to road conditions out ahead, local sights, personal history. People like to talk, and if they feel at ease they'll talk about themselves.

But people make up only part of a tour. The terrain, the geography, the *place,* makes up much of the rest. Here one's choices are limitless. Once restricted to paved or hard-packed roads, all-terrain bicycles (ATBs, or "mountain bikes") have now opened the remainder. On thin-tire bikes I've visited the pyramids, pedaled through Bombay, cycled Kenya and the islands of Japan. Then came fat tires, and the dirt road and trail excursions into the countryside. Days of sandstone labyrinths in our Southwest, cold nights spent in thirsty deserts, elk bugling their reveille in a mountain dawn—ATBs now offer the backpacking experience *minus* the God-awful weight of the backpack.

People. Places. The mobility to move quickly, easily, inexpensively, healthfully, between. Is there any wonder that some of us get hooked?

If it's so easy, so enjoyable, why is it that the only people seen touring are those struggling in summer's heat up mountain grades?

The answer to this oft-asked question is illuminating, for it has to do with the important issue of just what constitutes cycle touring. The first part of the answer is that such scenes of bikers toiling up hills is memorable to motorists. The crucial second part is that these are the only easily identifiable tourers.

Pass a solo cyclist with a single bag of gear, and one assumes he's out for an afternoon; but if his tour is one of motels only, and if he's packing light, all his necessary gear can fit into a single pack. Drive by a couple breezing through the countryside with only tiny seat bags filled with rain gear and tools, and chances are you won't suspect they're pedaling toward reservations at a nearby resort. Or see a group of cyclists with only handlebar bags aboard. Unless you spy the accompanying van of tents and cooking gear you probably won't suspect an organized tour, where riders are freed from weight and pedal into a camp ready-made—tents in place and dinner on the stove.

The simple point is that all these examples are various forms of cycle touring. Some 600,000 Americans do it each year, spending at least one night on the road. Two million of us commute to work by bike. And another 27 million of us cycle without overnight stays, on the 10 to 15 million new bikes sold annually (and on millions of older rigs).

Unfortunately, most of these cyclists are written off by "the biking world"—by magazines devoted to racing, acrobatic log jumping, and herculean rides; by books that profess "touring" as their goal but then concentrate on speed, on technique, on melding the two "machines" involved—the body and the bike; by cycle shops whose salesmen know all the finalists of last year's *Tour de France* but couldn't begin to tell you where to find a topographical map, much less read one.

It's a pity. Somehow the "no pain—no gain" lunacy, which isn't even physiologically correct, has made a successful long jump from Olympic racing to the touring world. People read of long daily mileages and even longer hours, of tough training and special clothes and high-carb diets, and they think this must not be for them.

It is time to change all that. I think it can be done simply, by the substitution of a single word, a word found in the subtitle of this book. For the next few chapters, try reading "travel" in place of "tour."

What is the difference? Just this. A lot of folks think there's only *one* way to bike tour. But everyone knows that travel is as personal as the traveler.

Beyond that, delightful images come to mind when the word "travel" is heard: pretty scenery, long meals, interesting people. In fact, the only drawbacks one hears about travel is, first, that it's expensive, and, next, that one returns out of shape.

But traveling on two wheels removes both those limitations.

It is almost time to get you on the bike. First, a final suggestion.

Try to remember, as you read the complex chapters that follow, the simple pleasures of bike touring I've alluded to above. Keep them in mind as an antidote to the confusion that can come from gear charts and Gore-tex. As someone who is trying to prepare you for the road I feel responsible to let you know the choices—the ways in which wise planning and a solid bike can make a good tour even better.

But don't lose track, when I'm waxing on about a modern-day eighteen-speed aluminum beauty, of the fact that the quality of a tour is not, ultimately, determined by equipment. True travel enjoyment depends upon your attitude, the places you visit, and the people you meet.

1
Selecting
a Bike

It used to be easy. In the America of Frigidaires and evenings spent around the radio one merely entered a bike shop, straddled the latest model Schwinn in his price range, paid the man cash, and pedaled out. Such simplicity.

But before you begin decrying the loss of these uncomplicated times, recall what it was like to pedal those old bikes uphill. Forty-five pounds of steel and a single speed didn't make things easy. Of course, the huge whitewalled balloon tires, built-in battery light, and red-and-white streamers dangling from the handlebars made the effort almost (but not quite) worth it. What really made the awful weight and sawhorse handling acceptable was the fact that we didn't have a choice.

How things have changed! Today's visit to the bike shop is, by comparison, frightening in the number of choices it presents. Do you buy a sleek, quick racing bike? A more sturdy, thin-tire touring rig? A fat-tire ATB (all-terrain or "mountain" bike)? And once that decision is made, will your frame be double-butted? steel alloy? aluminum? carbon fiber?

Don't get frustrated. Remember what I said earlier, that the quality of a bike does not dictate the quality of the tour. You don't have to have the latest design and lightest weight to love your ride. But if you are going to buy a bike, or think someday about upgrading your present mount, a good *general* knowledge of the machine is of value. Learn the basics of bike anatomy now, and later technological advances (like frame composition and component design) will be much easier to understand.

THE FRAME

A bicycle's frame is its skeleton, the internal structure without which all the accoutrements of wheels, saddle, derailleurs, fenders, and the like would make up merely an unrecognizable parts heap. Unfortunately, since most frames look relatively similar from the outside, they are often overlooked by the buyer. And this is a shame. For just as well-developed muscles are useless when wrapped about a broken bone, even the best components can't do much for a crummy frame.

So what qualifies as "crummy?" Luckily, you won't find one in most good bike shops today. Head to a department store, however, and you'll see steel frames that were stamped out in thick flat sheets, then welded into tubes with a long seam down the middle. (The seam is usually easy to see, even beneath the layers of paint.) Granted, the result is a heavy-duty tube, able to withstand considerable mistreatment without fatigue if joined together properly. Tough and inexpensive, such a frame has only two real problems. First, it weighs as much as a horse. Second, it rides like a dead one.

It is true that only four or five pounds separates the weight of a ninety-nine-dollar special at the local five-and-dime and the carbon-fiber frame costing ten times as much. Most of us would choose to lose those pounds through dieting instead of dropping that much cash. But the critical point here is not

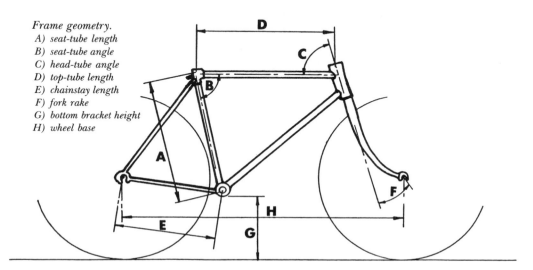

Frame geometry.
A) *seat-tube length*
B) *seat-tube angle*
C) *head-tube angle*
D) *top-tube length*
E) *chainstay length*
F) *fork rake*
G) *bottom bracket height*
H) *wheel base*

total weight. Too-heavy a frame is sluggish in acceleration and slow in handling, no matter what the rider weighs. Let us see, then, what is available between the extremes of too-heavy and too-expensive.

The next step up from rolled steel is a frame whose tubes are formed through the piercing of a long metal block, thereby forming a tube without seams. As the resultant seamless tube is inherently stronger it need not be as thick; that is, the "walls" of the hollow tube are thinner. Move one step farther to the use of a steel alloy (a mixture of two or more metals), and the result is another increase in strength and a decrease in weight. Now take another leap, to the increase of tube-wall thickness where stress is greatest (at the ends), and the thinning of those walls toward the middle. Such tubes are known as "double-butted," while those with the same tube-wall thickness throughout are termed "straight-gauge."

Don't get mad at me for going into this detail. I could simply suggest a couple of good bikes in each price range and style and move on from there. But it wouldn't be much help. Why? Because most values in the marketplace are fluid. This year the dollar is strong, next year the yen is rising, now the English pound and deutsche mark take a beating. . . . Situations change, and by the time you read this my suggested "best buy" may no longer qualify. So persevere in learning just these basic points, then shop around. The bucks you save will have bought this book and paid you a handsome wage for reading it.

Back to the basics. We've moved from seamed to unseamed tubing, to steel alloy in place of steel, to double-butting for strength and even lighter weight. Only several years ago I'd have mentioned aluminum frame sets as a very expensive option for shaving ounces and improving "stiffness"—the quick-response/lack-of-lateral-sway-when-pedaling feel to a bicycle's ride. But the price of aluminum tubing has now come down considerably, and with its fall this frame enters our list of "possibles." (One can hope, though perhaps not expect, the more exotic compositions of titanium and carbon fiber someday to come into the tourer's range.)

We now know enough about tubing to begin the pursuit of a bike. Rule One in this chase is to proceed *slowly*. Wait until the first warm snap of spring to start shopping, or decide only a month before a tour that you want a better bike, and chances are good that you'll end up with less than the perfect purchase. For heaven's sake, and your own satisfaction, realize the sophistication of these machines, and leave your wallet at home when you start making the rounds of cycle shops. The bikes are so pretty that you'll have to force yourself into comparison shopping.

In fact, I would suggest you buy a few cycle magazines (names in Appendix D), to read the ads and articles of most recent entries in the field. Each bike advertisement has an address for catalogues; write to those of interest. If you have questions, ask them. You'll be amazed at the in-depth and personal answers. And after you have finished this chapter you'll also be amazed at how much help each company's catalogue is to you, especially the "spec (specifications) chart," which provides information on type of tubing, derailleurs, gear pattern, and so on.

Let's pretend that the first spec chart you read (or salesman you meet in a shop) describes the frame as "Reynolds 531, double-butted main triangle." What is being said? You already know one of the terms (double-butted), and that you're talking strong, light tubing. The "Reynolds 531" part also refers to something already discussed, in that this is a very high quality alloy. (The "531" once referred to the ratio of manganese, molybdenum, and carbon in the frame.) Most good-quality alloy frames today are chrome-molybdenum (commonly referred to as "chro-moly" or "chro-mo") or molybdenum-manganese, and are manufactured under many names—Columbus, Ishiwata, Tange, Reynolds, Vitus, and more. (These names, and/or frame construction and composition, often appear in decals on the bike. "High Tensile" and "1020 Steel" indicate lesser quality than "chro-mo," and should be reflected in a smaller price.)

What about "main triangle?" That is the easiest of all. Look at the bike frame drawing and you'll see the three main tubes that form a kind of triangle—top, down, and seat tubes. Some forks, seat tubes, and chainstays are also butted, but *not* if (1) the spec chart or decal states "main triangle," or (2) only the words "double-butted" are seen. The point here is that bikes that are "double-butted throughout" almost always trumpet that fact clearly, as a matter of pride and justification for the price tag. ("Main triangle" implies the existence of another one; take a second look at the drawing and you'll see it—made up by the seat tube, seatstays, and chainstays.)

That takes care of the tubes themselves. Now we must put them together.

We have to return to our department-store bottom-line bike to find the worst manner of attaching tubes to one another. Look closely at the cheapest of these and you'll find that holes are cut, tubes inserted, and both affixed by a sloppy welding job. Moving up a notch, lugs (metal sleeves or fittings to cover these joints) appear, adding their strength as a "butting" for each tube. On some expensive bikes lugs are a thing of beauty, designed for the best in both form and function. But on cheap machines they serve only to cover up a lousy tube connection.

The tube ends of a good bike are mitered (cut or beveled to a specific angle) so as to fit together perfectly, and then brazed, not welded. Brazing, which takes place at considerably lower temperatures than welding, does not fatigue or make brittle the surrounding metal. Tubes connected perfectly in this manner are seen in some models without lugs at all, and such precisioned joints have proven their ability to handle rough treatment. However, most alloy touring bikes will be lugged, and it is important that you look at these tube junctures closely. Very sloppy work can be covered up easily with a lug. Name-brand bikes seldom make it out of the plant with such problems, but close scrutiny of lugs isn't a bad idea. Look for a constant, smooth flow to the brazing, and if there is any doubt you might remove the seatpost and put a finger inside. Only extremely sloppy work can be noticed in this manner, and some imperfections can escape detection by even the most critical observer. But at least you'll have put probability on your side.

Beyond the mechanics of *how* tubes are connected is the matter of *where*—at what specific angles—they are joined. Here we have reached the extremely murky waters of frame geometry. If you thought things got dark during the discussion above, you should try a few frame-design manuals as bedtime reading.

Unfortunately, such seemingly esoteric matters as chainstay length and head-tube angle play a big part in determining a bicycle's "feel." That is, does it handle like a quarter horse or a limo? Is the ride harsh, like that in a sports car, or as smooth as in a sedan? And which is best for touring?

Once again we must remind ourselves that "cycle touring"—traveling on a bike—must be seen as including a very disparate group. "The" touring machine for my kind of rides might well *not* be the best for you. Because I spend months each year in the saddle I don't want a harsh-riding, skittish bike requiring constant steering attention. My preference is that fine line between a stiff frame (little lateral sway when pedaling, and thus an efficient transfer of power) and a smooth ride. I want to be able to ride loosely with my hands easy on the bars, and the bike—like a trained horse heading back to the barn—able to deal by itself with bumps and blasts of wind.

You might want the same, or something for shorter tours, which handles more like a racing bike. Determining which you prefer will take some time, and some test riding of various bikes, but that's the easy part, for you've already made the crucial discovery that different rides are available.

You can cut down the number of bikes you will want to test ride by understanding just a bit about frame geometry. First, take a long look at the illustration on p. 00. It should be easy to see that (1) if the seat tube is too long your feet won't reach the pedals, and (2) if the top tube is too long the handlebars will elude your grasp. We will get into this more when we discuss frame "fit," but I mention it now to introduce the "seat tube angle" (produced by the meeting of seat and top tubes). Most touring bikes have seat tube angles of 72 to 73 degrees, with long chainstays (normally in the 16¾″ to 18½″ range), head tube angles of between 72 and 74 degrees, a sloping front fork, and a relatively long wheelbase (40+″).

Many books provide page after page on geometries, and I've done so myself in other works. But almost every reader I've heard from does one of the following. Either he or she skips the frame-design section entirely and surrenders to the manager of a bike shop (*usually* a good idea, as most owners/workers at shops are bikers themselves, know their products well, and want you as a satisfied, returning customer), or he and she look at the range of "common" angles and tube lengths and test out bikes accordingly. (Note: The entire biking world appears recently to be moving toward "harsher"—steeper—angles. This means simply that the head and seat tubes are more upright, that the wheelbase is a bit shorter, that the ride produced is "stiffer" overall. While touring bikes of late have grown only slightly more steep, mountain bikes have changed dramatically in this direction since their first appearance not many years ago. Pick up the specifications charts of many bikes and you will notice that touring and mountain bikes alike fall into a realm of common angles. Now don't get confused; once again this means only that the frame tubes of most models these days come together in roughly the same manner, producing similar wheelbases and roughly equivalent head and seat tube angles. Glance at the photos of the ATB and touring bike; do you see the far less steep head and seat tubes of the touring bike? In the shop you'll hear the words "shallow" and "relaxed" used for these touring bike angles.

Frame
A) *head tube*
B) *top tube*
C) *seat tube*
D) *down tube*
E) *bottom bracket*
F) *fork*
G) *seatstay*
H) *chainstay*
I) *dropout*

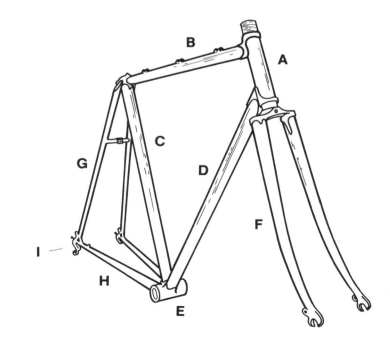

Ask the salesman in a good shop to put you on a bike which does *not* fall into today's common angle realm. Then pedal several "sport touring" models—the half-step classification between racing bikes and those designed for long loaded tours, and after this move to a full-on touring rig. Better than becoming confused with explanations of "trail" and "fork offset," you'll feel the difference between a racing bike's steeper angles and the relaxed, more shallow touring range.)

Now you're in the shop selecting models with well-built tubes, connected properly and at "touring" angles. Once the kind of ride produced by the frame is learned (usually obvious after just a few blocks of pedaling) move onto a quiet, level street or parking lot. Coast at a slow speed and remove your hands—but only a slight distance from the brakes. How does the bike handle by itself? If it is out of alignment—that is, if the frame is put together incorrectly—it will pull to one side or the other. The bike is "tracking" improperly.

This is also the time to notice the "skittishness" mentioned before when describing the ride produced by a racing bike's steep angles. Keep in mind that you are looking not for what feels good for a few blocks only, but for qualities that will not tire you over the long haul. More shallow angles will demand far less attention to steering; a longer wheelbase will soften the ride.

What about frame *style*? Fortunately, we are beyond the days of "boys'" and "girls'" bikes, determined by the presence or lack of a top tube. A touring load puts enormous stress upon a frame; the main triangle is of course greatly weakened if the top tube is not present. Some women might prefer a "mixte" frame (top tube sloping downward toward the crankset) for around-town riding, as it allows a skirt to be worn. But every woman I've met on the road has chosen the far stiffer "boy's" style for the tour.

HANDLEBARS

One of the greatest selling points of mountain bikes to older riders is the "upright" handlebars. People talk of not having to endure the foreign, paperclip curl required by "drop" bars. ATBs do allow a straight-back, George-Washington-in-the-saddle kind of ride, but the bars are not the reason. It is actually the far more relaxed angles of mountain bikes—shallower seat and head-tube angles—that produce this stance. (Although this is changing somewhat, ATB design calls for sloping seat tubes so as to put the rider's weight over the rear wheel, thus gaining critical off-road traction. Later trends have been to steeper angles for faster handling, requiring the rider to shift his weight backward in the saddle for uphill traction.)

But if one knows the various riding positions offered by the traditional

 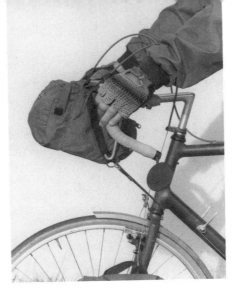 

Full curl position (#1 below). *Half curl position (#2 below).* *Upright position (#3 below).*

"drops" of standard touring bikes, a far more relaxed riding stance can be enjoyed. Granted, you will not be *as* upright as with upturned bars, but then there are advantages to a slightly forward lean. Leg muscles work more efficiently; arm, shoulder, and neck muscles are in good position for "pulling" the bars toward you while pedaling; wind resistance is reduced.

Drop bars offer at least three riding positions:

1. Full curl (or "tuck")—hands on lowest part of the bars, for greatest pedaling and braking power and least wind resistance.

2. Half curl—hands on brake levers (preferably "hooded" in a cushioning of rubber or other material), for good power, reduced wind resistance, fairly upright position, and safety of good grip on bars and fingertips on brakes.

3. Upright—hands close together next to stem, for most upright stance; problems with this are little bar control and longer reaction time if braking is required.

I find I'm in position number two always when in traffic, and almost always on the road. Very few mountains require me to drop into a full tuck, no doubt because my desire is not to race to the top but to see the world along the way. I occasionally drop into full curl when coming down a grade, when wishing greater speed. (You'll soon learn how to use your upper torso as a third brake, rising into half curl so that wind resistance can slow you down.) Very, very seldom am I in position three, that which so many tourers say they find necessary to avoid back and neck strain.

I avoid the pain, and the need to assume the least safe of these positions, first by making sure my brake levers are mounted high on the curve of my bars, and next by tilting my bars up slightly. It is not so efficient a position, but that's correct thinking only on the drawing board, or in wind tunnel tests. Anything in touring that can increase my comfort greatly, and reduce my speed only slightly, is far more efficient *over the long haul.* I'll stay in the saddle much longer each day if I'm comfortable.

GEARING

Frame and handlebar style are a bicycle's most obvious features. Next in order of importance to most people is the first question asked in the bike shop: "How many gears does it have?" The answer is easy—one, three, five, ten, twelve, fifteen, and eighteen—determined most often simply by multiplying the number of freewheel (the "cluster" of sprockets on the rear wheel, named for its ability to spin independently of the wheel) cogs by the number of front sprockets (chainrings). But touring cyclists mouth a close variation of this query that is far, far more difficult to answer: "How many gears do I *need*?"

To a degree it depends upon your kind of touring. In a later chapter, when all-terrain (mountain bike) touring is discussed, I will suggest a "triple crankset" (three chainrings, thus fifteen or eighteen gears) as mandatory. For pavement riding, however, I find such a simple answer far more difficult. The reason is that one's gear "range" is at least as important as the number of gears. Let me therefore explain the confusing numbers you will find in the spec charts, by borrowing a few paragraphs from my first book on the topic.

> Many bike manufacturers publish literature on their cycles stating something like "33 to 101 gear range as equipped," or "100 inch gear high range." What is a 100-inch gear, and how is that number derived? It comes from this formula:
>
> $$\frac{\#\text{ teeth in front sprocket}}{\#\text{ teeth in rear sprocket}} \times \text{wheel diameter in inches}$$
>
> Take my touring bike, for example: the large front sprocket has 54 teeth, the smallest back sprocket has 14.
>
> $$\frac{54}{14} \times 27 = 104 \text{ inch gear}$$
>
> But this does *not* mean the bike will travel 104 inches down the road with one pump of the pedals. It refers instead to the number of inches in diameter the front wheel would be in a "direct-drive" setup, such as

the old "high-wheelers" of the 1870s and 1880s. Those bikes had no complicated gearing, and therefore the single "gear" was determined by the size of the front wheel, to which the pedals were attached. Imagine a high-wheeler 104 inches in diameter, or more than 8½ feet high!

On the other end of the scale the lowest gear on my bike is 33.3 inches:

$$\frac{42}{34} \times 27 = 33.3$$

In this case the "high-wheeler" wouldn't be so high at all, and would look more like a child's tricycle. Now you can see the beauty of today's gearing, which provides for such extremes of great speed and hill-climbing potential, and all the ratios between.

I know it's confusing. But you can make things far easier by looking closely at a bike. Imagine the chain affixed to the largest chainring, and the smallest freewheel cog (thus the "highest"—hardest—gear). Let's assume the chainring is three times the size of the rear cog. In this case, each time the pedals revolve once (that is, each time the chainring is turned one time) the rear wheel will spin around three times. How far will that propel you down the road? That's easy, even without resorting to higher mathematics. Using a standard 27″ diameter wheel, we merely multiply this diameter by pi to obtain the circumference, then multiply again by three revolutions.

$27'' \times 3.14 = 84.78''$ (or about 7 feet for one revolution)
$7' \times 3$ revolutions $= 21$ feet

Now, imagine the chain on the smallest chainring and the largest cog in rear. Many triple cranksets have sprockets as small as and even smaller than the largest freewheel cog, but for our dicussion we will imagine they are identical in size (possessing the same number of teeth). In this case (a one-to-one gear ratio), each time the rider pedals once, the rear wheel revolves only once. And from the figures above we already know the bike would proceed only seven feet forward.

It stands to reason that moving seven feet with each pedal revolution would be far easier than propelling oneself twenty-one feet. When going uphill, therefore, and interested more in being able to continue pedaling than in covering distances quickly, we switch into our lower (easier) gears. When the summit is attained, or on the flat with wind at our backs, the relative ease of pedaling and our gear options allow us to take advantage of the situation by switching into high (harder) gears. Think of hiking up a hill, when you take short steps, compared to your long, easy strides on level ground. The principle is the same.

I received many interesting and informed letters from readers of that earlier book. One rider asked why I didn't drop my smallest cog on the freewheel to a 13 (thirteen teeth), thus allowing me to reduce the size of my larger chainring and shave a couple of ounces? The answer was that I had tried it, and I found that thirteen-tooth cogs wore out faster. (The difference would not be perceived by the average cyclist, but because I spend so much time on the road it became a noticeable problem.)

Another reader wrote to suggest that he'd figured out my "gear pattern"—the "gears" or "speeds" produced by each chainring when used in conjunction with each of the freewheel sprockets (extremely easy to do with the "gear charts" in the appendix), and determined that I had "overlapped" (duplicated) gear ratios in several instances. In effect, he said, I was riding a seven-speed bike. I wrote back that I shift, as do most tourers, almost throughout the range produced by my larger chainring, then I drop into the smaller ring for toughest hills. Granted, it is not the suggested shifting pattern, as it fails to make use of all possible gear ratios and creates more wear on the chain and sprockets. This additional wear is caused by the harsh angles produced by keeping the chain on the larger chainring while moving across nearly the entire freewheel width. But it is, for me, a far more natural way of shifting to meet changing conditions, requiring only seconds with a single hand and almost no thought whatever. (I do refrain from the *most* extreme "cross-chaining," a condition which results when the chain is on the largest chainring and largest freewheel sprocket, or on the smallest chainring and smallest freewheel sprocket. This is especially important due to developments over the last few years of triple cranks, extremely large and small chainrings, and six-sprocket freewheels with widely different-sized cogs.)

Many of the more mechanically inclined will jump on this lack of thought as the basic problem, but I'm not in the saddle to search for optimum ratios. Believe me, this is not a backhanded slap at the "engineer approach" to the world. My only point is that I usually find such people working happily as mechanics ("wrenches") in bike shops or training for a weekend race—not out on tour. My poor mind simply isn't able to handle computations of ratios and wind speed while I notice the world around me. For hours I imagine the countryside as it was in another geologic age, or the lives of those I've met in conversation in the last small-town café. Anything that gets in the way of such touring nuances is—for me—part of the load I jettison my first day on the road.

But back to readers' comments and questions. Most common of all, in terms of gearing, has been: Should I spend the extra money for a triple crankset? As this is years later, the first part of my revised reply must be that there is no longer such a wide disparity in price. Second, changers (derailleurs by an older name) have improved so much that the earlier problems of derailleur cage noise (produced by the chain rubbing against the inside or outside derailleur arm) are almost nonexistent. Third, and most important, is the consideration of the wide-ranging gear options that three chainrings provide.

I do not go along with the increasingly popular practice of greatly reducing the largest chainring on a triple, partially compensating by dropping the freewheel from a fourteen to thirteen smallest cog, selling a bike with a relatively low highest gear (less than 100), and telling the buyer that "increased spin" at lower gears is the correct way to ride. (More on that subject in a later chapter.) But I am completely and always in favor of *options* for a touring bike. (And for the touring *biker*. The unknown experience out ahead is, after all, one of the greatest attractions in two-wheeled travel.) One of my favorite touring rigs is a triple with a gear range from 25 to 112 (chainrings of 54/44/28; freewheel of 13 to 30). I use low end gears to save my knees when pulling grades with lots of weight, the high end to take advantage of tail winds after a good night's rest. (The extra-high range provided by the 13-tooth freewheel cog makes up for its tendency to wear out a bit faster, and I simply begin all cross-country rides with a brand new sprocket.)

Chances are you won't require this high a range, but don't hamstring yourself by buying one too low. Chainrings and freewheel cogs—unlike a poor frame—can be modified. If we were together at the bike shop I would push you toward ten speeds minimum (two chainrings; five sprockets in the freewheel cluster), a crankset with detachable chainrings (to facilitate inexpensive changes), and a wide gear range. In this manner you could always alter your gear pattern to suit your taste. (Remember that the pattern you prefer will likely change as you grow stronger.) Buy a three-speed and you're stuck for life with only three—a not-so-wide range and none of the choices in between to match all the changing conditions of touring. The final beauty of derailleur systems over hub-type three-speeds is that all the mechanical apparatus is in plain view and easy to master; three-speeds are for watchmakers, not for the rest of us.

Closely related to the discussion of gearing is derailleur shifter placement. I prefer mine on the down tube, no doubt because of years of habit but also because the hand falls naturally to this point when removed from the bars. It also assists in positive shifting (the sure, precise feeling of one's derailleur moving correctly into place), as the length of cable between shift lever and derailleur is the shortest of all alternatives. Other options are "bar-cons," where the shift levers stick out of each handlebar end, and the increasingly uncommon "stem-shifters," located on either side of the head tube. My problem with bar-cons is the relatively imprecise feel to the shifting, while I find the stem location difficult to reach.

A final placement option is that required by mountain bikes, where hands must be able to grip the bars, be near the brakes and to shift—sometimes all at practically the same time. I've seen a few thin-tire touring bikes modified by their owners to accept the ATB "thumb-shifters," but I didn't care for the feel.

*Bar-end or
bar-con shifters.*

First, I didn't see the need, and second, I found them in the way of my hands on the bars.

Beyond placement of shifters is the 1987 rage of "click-shifting"—the movement of the gear lever until a "click" is heard, rather than judging when the derailleur has changed gears by the feeling transmitted through the gear lever, your feet on the pedals, and the sound of the chain engaging sprocket teeth. In comparison to this "manual-transmission" system, SunTour's "AccuShift" and Simano's "SIS" systems of indexed shifters allow for smooth, sure, quick gear changes. This is especially valuable when in hilly country, when traffic noise is such that you can't hear your chain, and on a mountain bike all the time. (You won't be able to hear the click in heavy traffic. But I've found my hand quickly learns the distance necessary to move the gear lever, and I can always drop my eyes to the lever to move it to the next line or index; these are painted on some levers and represent one gear change each.)

I have traveled too few miles with these systems to write of their long-term durability, but both companies have been extremely open in discussing first-generation design modifications. Problems appear to have been eliminated, and my guess is that in a short time such systems will be expected on a bike as standard equipment. At this point my final consideration would vanish—the fear of sophisticated gear breakdown with only a poorly stocked small-town bike shop nearby. (Both SunTour and Shimano systems allow a flick-of-the-wrist reversal to the old-style friction shifting.)

TIRES

Almost all thin-tire touring bikes, except for extremely small frame sets for exceptionally short riders, come equipped with the standard 27″ diameter wheels. (Standard for mountain bikes is the 26″ diameter, but more on this in the ATB chapter.) Most riders settle for whatever tires happen to be on the bike when they buy it. Changes can be made at the time of purchase, however, with little increased expense, for you are in a good position if you present such alterations as necessary to the sale. Simply negotiate the cost of such an upgrade with the salesman, not forgetting the shop's time involved in making the change and the relatively low value of "stock" tires.

If you are buying a good machine the tires will probably be adequate. My personal preference in this area is a high-pressure, Schrader-valved 27 × 1⅛ clincher. Let's break this down in pieces.

"High pressure" refers to "psi"—pounds per square inch—capacity. The higher the pressure the easier the pedaling, but we pay for it in a harsher ride and increased tire wear. I split the difference here with 90 or 95 psi tires; anything less than 90 psi (in such a narrow tire width) seems to have difficulty handling my body, bike, and touring-load weight.

There are two types of tire valves—Schrader (like the ones found on automobile tires, most mountain bikes, and almost all bikes sold in America before the mid-seventies), and Presta. People talk about the mechanical advantages of Presta valves: that they require less effort to inflate, add less weight to the wheel, and require a smaller-diameter hole in the rim (due to this valve's slimmer profile).

Schrader valve.   *Presta valve.*

I can't say anything against those arguments. In fact, one of my touring bikes came equipped with Presta valves, and I've left things that way. It required only that I change one of my air pumps (a three-minute job, as they come with simple adapter kits), and that I pack along a very small brass "valve adapter" if I wish to air up at a service station. (One can go to the expense and bother of having rims drilled out for the larger Schraders, but this to me seems extreme.)

So why is my preference still Schrader? Sloth, pure and simple. The *only* time I use a hand pump is when a flat tire forces me into it, and I don't like the extra thirty seconds required to locate and screw on the Schrader fitting around my Presta valve. My preference is to pull into a gas station, ask the attendant if I can have some air, and, if he appears congenial, to talk about the town. Needless to say, I choose a station that isn't busy. Bikers don't endear themselves when their rigs prevent paying customers from getting to the pumps.

On to my preferred tire size of 27 × 1⅛. I have already indicated that 27″ is standard diameter for touring wheels. At all times, when possible, I choose "standard" features, as I might need repair or replacement parts many hundreds of miles from home. Tire widths (and heights, as the measurement refers to both dimensions) of 1¼″ or 1⅛″ are most common, and the differences between them are so slight as to be unnoticeable to me. The slimmer 1⅛″ tires hold up well for me on the road, however, and as they weigh a bit less I choose them when the 1¼″ original equipment tires wear out. (One-inch-wide tires exist, but they feel too narrow for me when I hit the occasional patch of sand or gravel on a road surface. Thinner tires, of course, handle such debris more poorly, and the decreased height means that one's rim is more likely to be damaged by chuckholes. These extremely narrow tires are just a bit too delicate for the abuse provided even when I'm riding carefully.)

Differences in weight are in this case very small, but whenever one can reduce his "rolling weight" without compromising wheel strength he should do so. "Rolling weight" refers to those grams that must be pushed both in a circle (the wheel and crankset) *and* down the road (oneself, one's load, the bike). For this reason, when cycling in desert or urban areas, I employ "tire liners"—optional plastic sheathings that one can install between tube and tire—rather than the heavier old standby of puncture-resistant tubes. Cactus needles, glass, and nails enjoy attacking tires, but I've cut down my punctures to about one per year by using "Mr. Tuffys" (only one of the brand names of tire liners).

"Tire savers" are thin, triangular metal bales that attach to the brake bolts and rest lightly upon the tire. The purpose, of course, is to pluck out anything one rolls over before it embeds itself in the rubber. "Savers" are inexpensive, and they work. But one can use them only if fenders are not present. And because I find dark streaks up my back and spray in my face embarrassing and uncomfortable, I opt for fenders every time. One other point: Only twice in all my touring—a Saint Louis-to-Canada ride in 1965 and a San Diego-to-Santa Fe journey in 1984—have I cut a tire so severely that even an inside "boot" (rubber patch) couldn't save it. Experience has taught me, therefore, that few tires require saving. Although savers do minimize the amount of road debris that succeeds in becoming one with your tubes, liners perform an almost perfect job of prevention.

The final term in my stated preference in tires was "clincher." One has two choices in tire types—clincher (wire-ons) and sew-up (tubulars). Clinchers are the tires we all grew up with, the kind with an easily removable tube and rubber-housed metal beading that "clinches" the wheel. Sew-ups have a tube sewn inside a tubular casing, making repair far more difficult. They are beadless, and are therefore glued or taped onto rims different in construction (no channels or "bead flange") from those made for the beaded clinchers. Used by racers for their extreme light weight (and use of lighter rims), ability to hold very high air pressure, and excellent transmission of road or track "feel," sew-ups are here to stay.

Some touring cyclists, concentrating upon the sew-ups' attributes for increased speed (and no doubt planning to perform the laborious repair later that night in camp), choose these far more delicate tires for long rides. But clinchers have made startling technological advances recently, putting them very close to tubulars in all categories. Air-pressure capacities of 125 psi are now available, and the metal beading in some is replaced by a Kevlar fabric, making these clinchers foldable. (A bike-shop owner in England taught me the "figure-eight" technique of folding metal-bead clinchers; see Chapter 2.)

Some clinchers also have a Kevlar or wire-mesh sheathing to ward off punctures (and therefore reduce the need for tire liners), and an extremely high "tpi" (threads per inch) body-casing count to provide for better handling and feel. And then there is the current battle between "slicks" and "herringbones," the companies that contend that the usual raised-center-bead/herringbone-side-pattern tread does not provide as little resistance nor as much traction as a completely bald tire surface. The jury is still out in this case, but most tourers at present are sticking with conventional tread designs.

Must we worry about it all? The answer is yes, if we wish to have the latest equipment and greatest advance in technology. Again, however, this is a book for that portion of the cycling world dedicated not to going farthest in the fastest time, but to wide-eyed travel. Give the arguments of "slicks" versus herringbone, high pressure and tpi, as much time as your bent toward the arcane allows. But beware the abyss reached when technological sophistication becomes sophistry.

SADDLES

Of the three rider/bike contact points (hands, feet, bottom), our well-padded posteriors stand first in line when it comes to memories of pain. Chafing of the loins, numbness of genitalia, saddle sores beneath the pelvic crests—any one of these maladies can ruin a tour. But before you decide to toss this book and take up squash, let me reassure you that there are remedies.

The first comes from saddle-design advances over the last decade. If you purchase a mid-priced touring bike chances are you'll get a padded, anatomically shaped, lightweight molded nylon saddle covered with a thin leather sheath. (Avocet is one, but only one, manufacturer.) The leather breathes, allowing perspiration to move away from the lower trunk. Padding eases the pelvic crest contact, while the thin nose of the saddle makes chafing a pain of the past. Unlike the next alternative, these padded nylon models do not "break in," but they do offer a very comfortable ride to both some cross-country bikers and, especially, the occasional Sunday cyclist.

A second major type of saddle, and the one preferred by many longtime tourers, is the all-leather style usually associated with the popular names of Brooks Professional or Ideale. Most of these when sold appear hard as a rock, and many times I've watched customers in a bike shop rap a knuckle on the saddle top and wince.

But these saddles do not *stay* hard. Their biggest advantage over the padded seats is the form they acquire as they soften up. You won't recognize it by sight, but that form is yours. And because it has molded to shape your body it is more comfortable than a pre-molded model could ever be. (More on this in Chapter 6.)

Other all-leather drawbacks often listed are required care, weight, and cost. As with all leathers, the animal that at one time moisturized his skin naturally has been removed; it is up to us as second owner/occupier to do this *un*naturally. The weight comes from the metal undercarriage and from the copper rivets holding the hide in place. The reason for greater cost is obvious, as top-quality metal and thick leather completely eclipse the plastics and hair-thin leather sheathing of their space-age cousins.

But are these really drawbacks? I have spent many evenings around a fire oiling the leathers of my touring kit—pedal straps, handlebar wrap, saddle, gloves, boots, knife sheath. Sometimes I've done this with tour companions; far more often it has been alone in camp, my ears attuned to the crackling of logs and hooting owls, and my thoughts on earlier generations. Man has ridden in saddles and ensconced himself in leathers for centuries, and at such times only my metal mount separates me from the Macedonians or Iroquois. Surely this, and the fact that leather saddles last nearly forever, justify a small increase in weight and cost.

Brooks Professional leather-and-copper-rivet saddle.

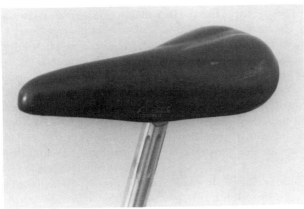

Avocet anatomic saddle.

I should add that this is an extremely personal position, one I hold as the owner of a soft, brown, aging, beautifully classic Brooks. It hurt me mightily at first, as I was dumb enough to begin a year-long ride with a brand new saddle. But that was *my* fault.

I won't consider it my fault if you go wrong in saddle choice, however, as I'm simply telling you my own experience and suggesting, if it is possible, that you try both styles. (Women tourers reading this should test the *women's* anatomic models, as the padded areas are farther apart to match pelvic differences, or the much wider Brooks B-72, if standard saddles don't seem to fit.) I doubt that any shop would lend saddles for as long a time as would be required to make a judgment, but you might ask a friend. Good luck.

Remember that no matter which kind you ultimately choose you'll have difficulty, on your first days of tour, if you don't keep your rear toughened through occasional rides. Work up steadily to long days on the bike. Everything on your body will appreciate it; your bottom, most of all.

BRAKES

If you think bike aficionados go nuts over the particulars of tire choice, you ought to see them when it comes to brakes. In one respect, however, the attention is appropriate. Although so many parts of a bike assist in quick acceleration or the ability to climb, brakes are *the* component designed to let you live to ride again.

Luckily, most brakes on most mid-priced touring bikes will do their job just fine. When the levers are squeezed the cable will tighten, pulling the metal arms of a side-pull, center-pull, or cantilever brake toward the rim. Rubber (or other material) pads or "blocks" will throw themselves against the spinning rims, in a desperate attempt to slow you down.

A sensitive rider will appreciate the effort. He will also recognize that no matter how valiant the brakes, the task is formidable. Enormous bike and rider weight increased by a touring load, rims that are often wet and slick, the stretching of cables, the wearing down and heating up of pads—brakes must overcome it all. And yet, when they've done it all and succeeded in slowing down revolving rims we still aren't satisfied. Lunge for the levers in gravel or sand, or grab them in a panic when the road is wet, and we blame the brakes when the bike just keeps on going. But the fault is ours, for not realizing that what ultimately slows a bike is the contact of tire rubber with the road. Even if the wheels are stopped, the bike can keep moving if we've ridden onto surfaces not intended for two wheels.

The point is evident: Riders have ultimate responsibility for slowing down. I'll deal with braking technique later (in tips for riding a loaded bike), and with maintaining cables and pads (in the chapter on repairs)—two areas in

Centerpull brake.

Sidepull brake.

which riders are often woefully deficient. This doesn't mean there aren't lousy brakes, inadequate in slowing rims even under the best of conditions. The problem comes in recognizing these before it is too late.

Once again you are in a good position simply by knowing you should be concerned. Next, as I've already mentioned, most touring bikes have good brakes. Companies do not set up bikes with good frame sets and derailleurs, then destroy the effect by hanging on bad brakes. So, to acquire the feel of both poor brakes and good, I suggest you spend some time first looking at and squeezing the levers of very low-priced bikes, then move up in grade. You won't have difficulty noticing the stronger grip required, lack of sharp mechanical response (a "mushy" feeling), inability to spring back to position, and less pad pressure against the rim provided by the cheaper models.

The three brakes mentioned above—side-pull, center-pull, cantilever—are all models of the single "caliper" style of brake. In each model metal arms are moved toward the rim, and it is in the method by which this action takes place that we see differences. The drawings will indicate the mechanical action in each; I'll simply add the following: First, some of the brakes in all three model groups will do a fine job of slowing down your wheels. Don't pass by a particular model, therefore, simply because you've seen a similar brake that didn't work. You will find that the brake pads on cheap (and I don't mean inexpensive) side-pulls won't spring back to clear the rim (one side rubbing slightly); that crummy center-pulls lose strength in metal arm flex; that the brazed-on posts (located on fork blades and seatstays, to which cantilever brakes are affixed) on poor bikes inhibit the cantilever action.

Some tourers feel that good-quality side-pulls (the choice of racers) are too sensitive to rim walls that are slightly out of true or dimpled by abrasion, unfor-

Cantilever brake.   *Roller cam brake.*

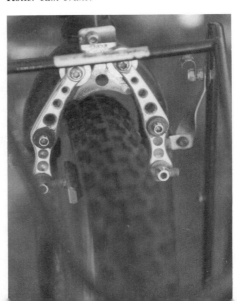

tunately so common in touring. By far the majority of touring bikes are now equipped with adequate finger-adjustable cantilevers or more forgiving side-pulls, however, so this is not a problem. I doubt if you'll find disc brakes at your local bike shop on anything but tandems, or power-cams and U-brakes on anything but ATBs (discussed later). You are therefore in pretty good shape simply by looking for the problems listed above, and by testing the brakes several times when out on a trial run. Make sure *before* you leave the shop, however, that your hands are large enough to span the distance between brake lever and handlebar.

OTHER ITEMS TO LOOK FOR

1. *Water bottle mounts.* Many bikes today come with holes already drilled into the seat and/or down tubes for bottle cages—a nice feature for which you'll pay a bit more, but not a necessity (I always have to add additional cages anyway).

2. *Fender/rack eyelets.* These not only make one's life much easier, but allow safe, secure attachment of accessories to the frame.

3. *Hooded-brake levers.* Rubber or other material covers for brake levers, making long days far easier on the hands.

4. *Quick-release wheels.* Not necessary, but a real convenience (unfortunately, also for a thief; when on tour keep your eye on the easily removed front wheel; when in town keep it locked).

5. *Pedals.* My preference is rat traps (corrugated edges), sufficiently wide to handle any heavy shoe or lightweight boot I might wear in winter, reflectors in front and rear, and toeclips and straps; cleats and the new "union" joints of Look-type pedals (where a device on the shoe bottom hooks into the pedal mold) make for efficient pedaling and impossible walking.

6. *Micro-adjust seatposts.* Easily adjusted from the bottom with a single allen wrench, these lightweight beauties also allow positioning at any angle a rider might wish.

7. *Braze-ons.* In addition to the water bottle, rack, and fender fittings mentioned above, one sometimes finds derailleur cable guides, brake cable tunnels, pump and chain hanger pegs (to hold chain when rear wheel is removed).

8. *Sealed bearings.* My personal preference in this category is a sealed-but-accessible bearing, for it is the best of both worlds—greater protection against water and grit than unsealed, yet, if necessary, the tourer far from home can

get into it for repair; some sealed mechanisms require a special tool for entry, which is fine if the tool is lightweight and small; ask the salesman to show you the tool, inquire about cost, listen to what he says about the lessened maintenance, and then make up your own mind.

9. *Skinwall tires.* I know we've spent a lot of time already on tires, but no matter which size or style you choose there's no reason to push around more weight than necessary; heavy gum tires slow you down, whereas skinwalls are far lighter and not that much more expensive.

10. *Alloy components.* Whether it's a crankset, wheel rim, brake, handlebar, or fork, steer clear of pure steel (except in axles, bearings, and races); heavy and dull when it comes to the ride, its presence on a bike should warn you to look out for similar poor features; you will find good-quality aluminum in place of alloy on some bikes.

11. *Multi-piece, five "pin" cotterless crank.* Two decades ago crankarms were held in place with cotter pins; removing the crank for bottom bracket bearing maintenance required the driving out of usually frozen cotter pins with a ball peen hammer, and sometimes a drill and blowtorch. Most good bikes today come with cotter*less* cranks, requiring only a wrench for removal. Be sure to look for this when you buy.

Multi-piece cranks allow you to change chainrings individually (an excellent and inexpensive way to alter one's gearing for particular terrains, or simply replace worn out rings), and without having to replace the crankarm in the process.

Look at the non-pedal end of a crankarm; if it's a good, recent-vintage bike you will find five "pins" radiating out to the chainrings. Less expensive bikes have only three such pins. A tremendous amount of pressure is exerted while pedaling, and five pins help to keep the chainrings true. On my older three-pin cranks I often developed a slight wobble, which caused the chain to scrape against the derailleur cage as it revolved.

12. *Low-flange hubs.* It is obvious that if the flange (the metal spoke housing surrounding the hub) is low, the spokes must be long. Likewise, the higher the flange, the shorter the spokes. I've heard some great arguments on the pro's and con's of low- and high-flange hubs, but it seems to me that high flanges require the resultant shorter spokes to attach to the hubs at a more severe angle. To my mind this is a drawback that could cause more spoke breakage, though I've never really tested the theory. It also appears that the longer spokes of a low-flange hub absorb road shock better than short spokes. Most bikes today come with low flanges.

13. *Deep color.* No matter what the color, it should possess a lustre or appearance of depth, indicating a baked-on quality or otherwise professional application.

14. *Solid feel.* As car buyers kick tires and slam doors, bike buyers often pick up bikes an inch or so and, while yet holding onto the saddle and handlebars, drop them rather gently to the floor; if the headset or other parts are loose you are likely to feel or hear it.

15. *True wheels/chainrings.* "True" refers to revolutions without wobbles back and forth; you can see these both in the shop and while riding slowly.

SIZE

Much of what has been discussed above is of critical importance in choosing the right bike. But it all pales in comparison with the importance of "fit." The reason is obvious. Even the best machine is of little value if it's a pain to ride. Fail to get good leg extension and you've robbed yourself of power. Buy too tall a bike and you'll know it when you come out of the saddle unexpectedly. Ride too long a bike and you won't be able to reach the brakes when you need them in a pinch.

Some bike shops are excellent at matching you to a machine. But remember the lesson you learn with shoes: Even the cobbler who makes them can't tell you which pair fits best. The salesman will probably begin by asking you your inseam, then having you straddle a bike that allows you one to two inches of clearance over the top tube. (I prefer one inch with thin-tire bikes, two inches when it comes to ATBs. Racing shops will tend to put you on far shorter frames, as racers save weight this way. Remind them that you plan to *tour*.)

After this comes saddle-height position, at a point where there's but a slight bend remaining in the leg when the pedal is at six o'clock (straight down). Racers wish less extension; tourers, more. Some people determine correct saddle-height position by placing the heel of the foot on the pedal, and making sure there's contact throughout the pedal rotation. Others work both ways from a figure of 109 percent of inseam length. And some even slip their feet into the clips, ride a bit, and see what height feels best while still allowing nearly full extension. My experience with new tourers is that saddles are kept lower at first, until riders feel natural on the bike, and then are raised a bit to allow for more extended "ankling" (discussed later).

Next is saddle fore/aft position, where it is slid upon its rails toward the handlebars or back until the middle of the knee is directly over the pedal when the foot is held at three o'clock. I advise approximations for personal comfort.

The lower torso is now happy, and we move upstairs. Top-tube length determines at what angle your poor back will ride when you're stretched out to the handlebars. Many shops will place the bars about an inch below the saddle height, then have you assume your normal riding position. (I prefer my bars even with the saddle top. And because my hands usually are on the brake hoods, that is the point from which I determine correct top-tube length.) They'll look at your back to find an approximate forty-five-degree angle, your arms to see that they can bend at the elbows, your face to see if it's reflecting pain from being stretched too far. Some will even drop a plumb line from your nose, hoping it falls about a half-inch behind the bars.

Many of you reading this will of course own bikes already, and might be crying because your frame's too short. Well, dry your tears. If the difference is only an inch or so your remedy lies in a relatively inexpensive longer stem extension. (Be sure, of course, to have the saddle in correct fore/aft position before determining this.) You can also gain a little height with a longer seatpost, and a wee bit with longer crankarms. But both present some problems. Try to extend a frame with too long a seatpost and you're thrown out of correct fit with the rest of the bike. Tall riders sometimes prefer longer crankarms, but thereby reduce their ability to pedal through even slight turns and leans (as the pedal/ground clearance is decreased).

Finally, ask the salesman to hold a rack and pannier in place over the rear wheel, slip your foot into the clip and see if your heel clears the bag. If the bike is short you might also at this point make sure the front wheel (add a bit for the fender) will clear the toeclip when the tire is turned.

The moral of all this is to take your time in determining both best fit and best bike. You won't feel completely natural on any rig until you've "personalized" things (correct saddle and handlebar tilt, favorite bar tape, pedal straps at the perfect length to let your foot in and out easily—subjects that I discuss in later chapters)—and have gotten used to the touch of new components. But don't rush it. It takes a while for any bike to acquire the easy-chair feel of a perfect touring machine.

2

Equipment for the Bike

Iᶠ ʏᴏᴜ ꜰᴏʟʟᴏᴡ ᴍʏ advice in the last chapter you'll be set up with a quick, nimble, lightweight bike for your very first tour. If you pay attention in *this* chapter you can start your two-wheeled career with gear designed to make it perfect for the tour. From fenders and pumps to racks and packs, I'll try to cover everything that attaches to a bike.

Next are the spare parts and tools, a seemingly boring topic that only comes to too-true life when there's trouble on the road. Give this list at least a cursory glance at present, but a long look shortly before the ride. It is silly, after all, to blow a day on tour because you forgot a wrench.

BIKE ACCESSORIES

Fenders

Compared to the metal fenders on the balloon-tire bikes of my youth, the newer generations of plastic wraps weigh next to nothing. Unfortunately, the stays (those gleaming stainless-steel arms that hold the fenders in position) are still metal, and therefore of noticeable weight. Fenders are also a pain in three other ways. First, they are easy to damage and always in the way when the wheel is removed. Second, unless one is careful the stays can be bent (when leaning the bike over, for example), or the small nuts and bolts that hold the

30

Right: A scene from my 1984 "March to the Sea" ride across Georgia. Notice the front low-rider Robert Beckman Designs (Needleworks) panniers, brake hood mount mirror, and riding flag.

THE MARCH TO THE SEA

On Nov. 24, 1864, the Left Wing of Gen. Sherman's army [,
which had left Atlanta on Nov 15th on its destructive March to
the Sea, crossed the Oconee River at Milledgeville enroute to
Sandersville. On the 26th, after delays caused by destruction
of bridges over Buffalo Creek by Wheeler's cavalry [, the Left
Wing (14th and 20th Corps -- Maj Gen H.W. Slocum, USA) reached
Sandersville, the 14th Corps (Davis) having marched via Black
Spring and the 20th Corps (Williams) via Hebron. Near Keg and
Buffalo creeks their advance had been hotly contested, but the
infantry columns forced back the small cavalry units and entered
Sandersville before noon. The invaders having been fired upon
from the windows and portico of the court house, Gen. Sherman
ordered the structure destroyed.

That afternoon, Jackson's and Geary's divisions, 20th Corps,
moved to Tennille (3 miles S) to destroy the railroad from that
point to Davisboro. Next morning, Ward's division, 20th Corps,
and Carlin's division, 14th Corps, moved to Davisboro with the
artillery and trains of both corps. Morgan's and Baird's divisions, 14th Corps, moved to Fenn's Bridge (13 miles NE), crossed
the Ogeechee River, then turned toward Louisville.

On the 27th, Gen. Sherman, who had accompanied the Left Wing
from Atlanta to Sandersville, changed to the Right Wing (15th
and 17th Corps) which was then near Tennille.

106-16   GEORGIA   HISTORICAL   COMMISSION   1957 stay and fender together work loose, bringing on rubbing of the fender and tire. Third, mud and snow can become packed so hard beneath a fender that all tire movement stops.

Yet despite these difficulties, far worse is the alternative of water and road crud up your back and front, all over your gear, and thrown into your brakes and derailleurs. Exercise some care to avoid damaging your stays, and use Loc-Tite or some other nut-fastening solution to keep from losing the small attachment parts. Concerning mud, what are you doing on a dirt road anyway? Those are made for ATBs, where alternatives of down tube–mounted splash guards and rear rack covers must sometimes replace fenders. And snow will clog only under extremely heavy, wet conditions, times when tourers usually (and judiciously) decide to remain in camp.

Mirror

You've got plenty of styles from which to choose, but choose not to ride with a mirror and you're just asking for trouble. Not only is it a pain to turn around all the time to eyeball traffic, but very few riders can do it without pulling their handlebars slightly to the left.

Those of you who wear helmets can use lightweight dental mirrors, which attach easily to the helmet. There are others that wrap around the left sidebar of sunglasses, some that attach by a velcro strap to the handlebars, and the best (in my opinion), which mounts above the brake handle. Naturally, the last model is the hardest to install. But it has sufficient pivot points and length to extend past any rider's left arm and flapping coat sleeve, and to give a big, clear view of the world behind.

I've tried the small dental mirrors and fault them in two ways. First, I want a mirror in place constantly, not just when I'm wearing sunglasses. (Granted, if one wears a helmet constantly the mirror would always be in place. But although I suggest helmets to every rider I never ride with one myself. My unsound, insufficient justification for bareheaded pedaling comes later.) Next, I can't see much of the world, or view it as easily, in that relatively tiny space.

A mirror is a touring necessity—for safety, and scenic second looks.

Bar-end mirror, handlebar suspension (notice aluminum support frame and tension strap).

Handlebar Tape

It hurts me to see the loud-colored, worthless plastic wrap on handlebars. Why? Because unlike automobiles, where anything is added without thought of weight or purpose, bicycles are supreme examples of the best in form and function. Bar tape looks good, even elegant, *and* serves the necessary function of absorbing perspiration from the hands, protecting them from the hot or cold metal, smoothing out shocks from the road. Plastic, on the other hand, has only its garish, peacock color going for it. And if we buy this junk it's only a matter of time before similar Detroit-style intrusions make their way into the industry.

Fortunately, it is an easy job to replace tape. For now I'll simply mention types. Cotton tapes of many colors are available in shops. You will find that manufactuers provide just barely enough to do the job (one roll for each side of the bars), especially if you begin your wrapping where I do—very close to the stem. Another, more recent, option is foam. This does the job, I guess, but it's got as much form as my attempts to ski. Then there's the wrap created by Spenco, a company whose products have brought many back to cycling by ending the pain sometimes associated with it. (Their sorbothane-filled gloves and saddle covers can be found in many shops, along with shoe orthotics to deal with instep pain.) The Spenco wrap slides onto the bars, and I find its blue color less offensive than foam.

Stem shifters; foam handlebar wrap; unsafe "safety bars."

But my choice, by far, is leather. It comes in black or brown, the latter aging into a rich, sweat-stained hue reminiscent of cavalry saddles that one sees in Civil War museums. It's elegant, functional, a link of past and present, and was once alive: an unbeatable combination.

Water Bottles/Cages

I have already mentioned that many bikes will have braze-ons for two or three cages—one on the seat tube, one on the top (rider side) of the down tube, and sometimes another below it. Those of us who ride large frames (my touring bikes are 25½″) are fortunate in having long tubes for mounting more cages; I've had as many as eight affixed for desert trips, including one behind the seat post. Granted, it looks funny. And even empty cages and bottles add up in weight (not like full ones, however; a gallon of water tips the scales at nearly *eight* pounds.) But I learned long ago in the Middle East that when it comes to water I would prefer to err on the side of excess.

I'll talk at some length later about the human's need for water, and discuss the quantities you might find that your hardworking body demands. I will also strongly suggest the pump-type water purifier I've now carried for several years (if you venture into all-terrain touring) and discuss its attributes in the ATB chapter. For now you should simply recall the last time you were very thirsty, then buy accordingly.

Note: Regular-size bottles carry twenty ounces of water; the larger ones pack twenty-seven. I therefore pack as many of the big ones as possible *unless* my tube length allows two short bottles, but has room for only one larger one. The reason, of course, is the thirteen extra ounces I get through a second smaller bottle. Also, I always carry at least one of the smaller versions. This is because of the number of shallow sinks in which the larger bottles just won't fit beneath the tap. In these cases I simply use my shorter bottle to fill my larger ones.

Reflectors

Some bikes come with reflector mounts that appear to have been designed for tractors. Made of stamped, low-grade steel, they more than equal the weight that that same company has so laboriously (and expensively) shaved from rims and components.

Then there are the pannier manufacturers who find it necessary to put reflectors on nearly every pack they make. Of course, it's a plus for safety, but when illuminated from behind, a touring rig with all those bags resembles a Mack truck. It may be *safe* overkill, but I don't like the unnecessary weight. I've also had two of these reflectors jar loose during rides, leaving a small round hole in my bag's Cordura nylon shell.

Head lamp.

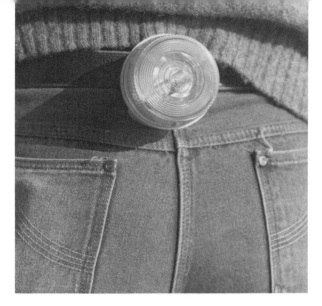

*Belt beacon—great
nighttime safety device.*

When commuting I want to look like a billboard, and I don't mind the weight. But for a tour I ride with only pedal reflectors front and rear, and one large red reflector mounted to the top rear of my back rack. (A safety study has indicated that motorists see best the moving pedal reflectors and those mounted high up on the racks. For this reason, even if your fenders come equipped with a reflector I suggest mounting a second on the rack.)

There are, however, times when nothing you can do will make for a safe ride. Even good generator lighting systems produce a puny beam in comparison to headlights; the car might see you but you'll be blinded by its lights and will not be able to see the road. Choose a campsite before dusk, if possible, linger over breakfast until the sun is up, avoid even walking on the shoulder when fog is thick. If I am forced to ride at night on tour I wear the headlamp for light, wear my yellow poncho if the heat isn't too great, ride slowly and as far to the right as possible, and pray.

Air Pumps

Packing these things can be a pain. Employ the frame mounts or braze-ons set along the top or seat tubes, and the pump can be stolen in a wink. The seat-tube location takes up critical water-bottle room; the top-tube placement makes lifting or carrying the bike extremely difficult.

My own solution is to slip the pump beneath the rack straps (bungee cords) holding the sleeping bag in place, or roll it inside my ensolite ground pad. After all, there's no real reason for the thing to be accessible.

Some of you might counter that you use them to ward off dogs. If so, you've chosen a poor weapon. Pumps are too short and too flimsy to pack much wallop, and far too expensive to replace. Besides, if you damage the pump on some poor mutt and then have a flat before the next bike shop you're really out of luck. And although improbable, you might just catch the dog in the eye with the bale device on the pump end. In the heat of attack one could care less how much damage is done to the attacker, but when heads have cooled hard feelings can result. I'd hate to think I'd caused some dog that much needless pain. My alternative, for protection of myself at the time and my conscience later, is the riding flag. (This and other options are discussed below.)

By the way—I know it sounds silly, but make sure your pump is in good shape before *each* tour. It may have worked like a champ when you put it away after your last ride, but gaskets can become dry and cracked. Also, make sure when you purchase your pump that it has the capability to replace all the air you need. A commuting pump can get by with only filling you up partially, as long as it's sufficient for you to reach the next bike shop or gas station in town. But on a tour the nearest air compressor can be a day away. The Zefal HP (high pressure) is not the only good pump made, but it is one of them.

An excellent air-pump alternative for commuting or the weekend tour is the tiny cartridge-operated QwikFil. On a long ride, however, you might need air more often than this unit would allow.

Kickstand

Not so many years ago I counseled against using kickstands on fully loaded touring bikes. The reason was that no stands on the market were long enough to keep a loaded bike sufficiently erect. A rider would think he'd balanced things perfectly, and then a gust of wind would come. BAM! A broken mirror, ripped stuff sack or pannier, or worse.

Today, thanks primarily to the much higher bottom brackets (that portion of the frame through which the pedal axle runs) of ATBs, longer kickstands exist. Buy a very long, lightweight (alloy) model, then hacksaw it if necessary to perfect length. With care you can then leave your bike upright on most surfaces, a position that is faster and cleaner and looks far better in photographs.

Riding Flags

The item on my bike that bothers the racing/fast-as-possible touring crowd the most is the riding flag. Why? You've got me, unless it has to do with the *un*sleek

A full touring load in the Rockies. Notice riding flag, brake mount mirror, folded clincher, kickstand, and pannier rain covers.

image it conveys. No matter that it weighs very little and is an extremely useful tool, or that it is a great safety device and adds a dash of color to one's photographs.

Unfortunately, this lack of acceptance by so many cyclists causes the supply and selection of flags to be erratic. You might have to look hard if you decide to give my preference a try. I like the orange, stiff-rod type, mounted on the left side of the front wheel. (The handlebar bag keeps it from blowing back into my face.) Mounting it in front makes boarding the bike as easy as when no flag is present, but more important is the fact that when a dog attacks I can simply snatch my flag from its aluminum holder and brandish the thing as a whip. It usually works; only a dozen times or so in all my riding have I had to wallop a hound, and when I do, the flag stings only momentarily. (Be *sure* to stop when a safe distance away from the dog to put your flag back into its holder. No matter how carefully you attempt replacement while riding, you stand the chance of driving the rod into your front spokes, causing a faceplant.)

Of course, one can use my urban, sometimes-solution to dog worries of full-strength ammonia in a water bottle, or a handlebar-mounted spray can of Halt! (brand name). But on tour I can't afford to give up that much water, and I would prefer not to run the risk of blinding the dog. He might run out into traffic, causing injury to himself or others. Besides, I try to choose gear that will at least do double duty.

Let me add one point here. I love dogs. I like cats, too, but I love dogs. They are often my sole source of tactile affection on a long tour. I can't blame the things for chasing a moving target; I'd do the same if my life consisted of scratching and eating and barking at the moon. Most times I can tell by the howl and tail-wagging if the dog means business; I often de-saddle to pet the thing. So it bothers me when fellow dog lovers misinterpret my words and write to me of cruelty.

I could respond that it is the duty (and the law) for dog owners to control their animals. But no one wants to have his hound leashed constantly, especially in the country. Thus it's up to the biker to protect himself not only against dog bite, but against being pushed—fatally, perhaps—out into traffic. No one should squawk when a rider chooses a *compassionate* weapon for self-defense.

Toeclips/Straps

Definitely. (See remarks in Chapter 1.)

Touring bike toe clip and strap; this model is bare metal and hard on the toes of leather shoes, but some clips have leather sewn around the metal for protection, and others are now made of plastic.

Hooded Brake Levers

Definitely. (See remarks in Chapter 1.)

Racks

I had one break on me once. I'll never forget the sound, or the sinking feeling I experienced as the heavily loaded rear carrier fell to the fender, pressing it down upon my tire and bringing me to a halt. It was early December, and I was nine hundred miles into a very cold ride along the Santa Fe Trail.

The lightweight, tubular aluminum-alloy rack had snapped at the point where it connected with the brake bolt. I'd questioned that juncture before I bought it, as it was the sole front-end support for the weight of my rear panniers, tent, sleeping bag, ground pad. But who was I to wonder? I'm not a designer, nor an engineer. Besides, it had stamped on it the biggest name in racks.

When it broke I of course worked myself into a huff, cursing everyone even remotely connected with that purchase except myself. Then, noticing the rack remained broken, I dug inside the panniers for my trusty shank of parachute cord, suspended the rack with it as best I could, and rode for the nearest Missouri town.

The world brightened. I met the nicest welder east of the Rockies, lingered for two hours over sweet rolls and coffee, watched him skillfully repair my rack in fifteen minutes, and was invited back for squirrel hunts in the fall. What a guy—and I'd never have met him except for metal fatigue.

Common-style (Blackburn type, though not Blackburn brand) rack.

One of many types of "rack-trunk" type bags.

This didn't mean, however, that the next time my rack decided to self-destruct I wouldn't be high in the mountains, toughing out a squall to make it into town. Or eighty miles from water in Nevada sand. And thus the need—the requirement—that my next "frame extension" be trouble-free.

Once again we bikers are in luck. Chro-moly racks (Bruce Gordon's) now exist, which look like pieces of sculpture, yet possess a tensile strength of 95,000 pounds per square inch and are as stiff and stable as your frame. The far less strong (and less expensive) aluminum-alloy racks have also made advances; the manufacturer of the rack mentioned (and cursed) above has replaced the fragile brake-bolt mount with steel. I've used both kinds of racks extensively and never had another problem.

At the far low end you'll find the kind I took around the world (there weren't many choices then), with moveable support arms and a spring-loaded top. These are heavy, and they sway in the breeze, putting enormous strain on the arms. They also connect to the seatstays with metal clamps that persist in slipping down toward the brake (some people use friction tape, a wood block, or hose clamps to fix this). But they are cheap.

The next step up are the many models of lighter aluminum-alloy, with three support arms reaching down on either side of the wheel toward a single-bolt connection. These are fairly stiff, and most have adequate brake-bolt or seatstay connections. (Front racks of this style usually have two support arms, and reach around the head tube to attach at the rear of the front brake bolt.)

Beyond choices of cost, attachment, and rack metal, a tourer planning long rides (necessitating a front rack to reduce weight on the rear wheel) must

State-of-the-art Bruce Gordon front rack; also notice roller cam brakes and "continuous-rubber" knobby tread pattern.

decide between a regular-height or a "low-rider" front rack. Manufacturers rave about the lowered center of gravity with low-riders, which provide increased stability in the front end. They have even taken this argument off-road, where one's increased stability is soon destroyed by the logs, rocks, and cacti one bangs about with the lowered front panniers. For touring bikes I can see this purpose, and agree that the world seems a bit more stable with one's front bags only inches above the road.

But I don't like low-riders. Often forced to ride with them while testing specific bike/pack/rack combinations for manufacturers, I sorely miss the storage capacity provided by a regular-height front rack. (This is where I prefer storing my spare clincher, and resting on top of it my vest and jacket in a small stuff sack. Without this convenient top of the front rack, these items must be added to the already high rear load, or crammed inside panniers.) I have two other complaints. One, I don't like having to bend down that low for access to my low-riding panniers (granted, a relatively minor matter). Two, I don't like the look—a major matter if the form or style of your touring rig is important to you. No doubt my preference for the look of leather saddles and high-riding saddlebags (my preferred term for panniers, by the way, and not to be confused with the little "seat bags" that suspend from the saddle) is due partially to my age; I grew up with them.

Spend some time choosing racks; the paragraphs above are intended to get across the message that all are not created equal, and to show you the result of a poor choice. Spend time, too, in mounting these racks properly. A bungled job of installing even the best rack will come back to haunt you. Bikers used to have to search for long, small-diameter bolts to fit frame holes, but now most racks come with bolts whose threads will match frame braze-ons or mounting holes. (Unfortunately, many of these tiny bolt heads—designed for a small allen wrench—are made of soft metal that "rounds out" if you're not careful. I always pack a couple of extra bolts if I'm preparing for a long tour.) Keep them from backing out of the holes (due to road vibration) by adding a drop or two of thread-locking compound.

Panniers

Back in 1965, on my first cross-country tour, my buddy and I carried most of our belongings in backpacks. A couple of weeks before the ride my partner had added heavy metal baskets, and I had found and purchased an extremely small pair of red-and-white plastic panniers. Into these we dumped many of our army surplus C rations and Sterno stove, and in this primitive state we made our ride. Not comfortably, mind you. But everything, after a fashion, worked.

Almost a decade later, on my round-the-worlder, another friend and I sported large rear panniers. If front racks existed at that time I didn't know about it; the result was that all our touring weight was over the rear wheels (which paid us back with seven broken spokes and two dozen flats). If better bags existed I was ignorant of that, too. Twice each day we laboriously grappled with the web-and-buckle attachments; the fiber board used as backside stiffeners broke, pushing the bag into the spokes; the fabric was such that our bag contents seemed to get wet whenever a cloud appeared on the horizon. Again, we made it. But not without discomfort.

And now another decade in development. The advance is amazing; it's like comparing mechanical pencils and word processors. Even the worst bag made today is far better than what I took around the world. And the other end of the spectrum—the "best" pannier? Well, they're beautiful to the eye, easy to mount, stable on the bike, quickly and easily accessible, and long-lasting. But they aren't cheap.

Between the two extremes of best and worst in bags you should have little trouble finding what you like. Use the following considerations as a guide.

Materials. Most bags today are made of various weights (thicknesses) of Cordura nylon. The thicker of these fabrics (8½ oz. per yard and 11 oz. per yd) are extremely abrasion- and water-resistant, the latter quality often enhanced by a urethane coating. Polyester thread, designed not to stretch, mildew, shrink, or break down due to ultraviolet radiation, is sometimes employed at eight to ten stitches per inch (double- and even triple- stitching at stress points). Self-repairing YKK zippers, heavy-duty nylon and polypropylene webbing, steel or tempered aluminum hardware, and metal or polyethylene unbreakable stiffeners round out the materials list on some of the best bags.

Front panniers—Beckman.

Construction. Some saddlebags are, in design, a rather simple sack. Others sport a number of outside zippered Cordura pockets, external open or zippered mesh pockets (excellent for drying clothes), lashtabs (to which one can "lash" equipment with optional webbing), snaps for mating with another pannier, and top web handles—both features to make carrying easier when the packs are off the bike. Some bags are large and rectangular in shape, and squared off on the bottom to sit upright for packing. Others are rounded at the base, thereby reducing the possibility that a combination of shorter chainstays and larger feet might cause a heel to catch the pack bottom on the upstroke. (Rectangular-bag manufacturers sometimes handle this problem by angling the bottom-front portion of their rear panniers.) Large, one-inch-wide zipper covers help keep water away from these areas most sensitive to foul weather.

Attachment. Most bags today have some kind of hook-and-spring support system, wherein two hooks on the upper back of each bag hold it aloft, and a bottom spring or tension strap keeps it close to the rack. Some add sophsticated locking devices, or employ webbing at the base for increased stability.

Fine. Now you can identify quality. But which of these good bags is for you? I've written before that beauty—and the "best" pannier—lie in the eyes of the beholder. My personal choice wouldn't help you, therefore, especially in that I have various preferences for my different kinds of rides. Most people must make do with a single set of panniers (usually two rear bags for short rides, four bags for longer trips), and make them last as long as possible. So, just as you did when choosing a bike—go slowly. Begin by writing to the pannier companies listed in Appendix E; request catalogues, and compare. Next, purchase a few bike magazines and request catalogues from any pannier companies not on my list. Visit *several* bike shops and look at what is available. And talk to bikers.

Your first and second considerations—what you will demand of a saddlebag and how much you can spend—will automatically steer you away from many. If you plan to tour a lot with heavy loads, or tour a little but want to be using the same bags twenty years from now, buy quality. Pay close attention to particulars, like the double and triple stitching and stitches per inch mentioned above. The heavier Cordura fabrics will last longer.

Now for what I find most important. First, of course, is *durability*. I don't want the hassle of broken zippers and dropped stitches thousands of miles from home. Next, I want *accessibility* to the bag's contents. And this automatically knocks out top-loading panniers for a tour. Why? Because the gear I carry on my racks sticks out and over the panniers, thereby making entry extremely difficult. When telling some bag manufacturers this I've heard the reply, "No, no. Tourers don't need access to the contents of their main compartments until they stop to camp. What they need during the day can be packed in the smaller pockets or front bags."

I don't agree. Furthermore, I think *they* wouldn't agree if they ever toured. First, the items on my front rack often stick out over the bag just as in back, meaning that I need front-loading accessibility there as well. Second, I need to get to food, clothing, books, notebooks, water purifier, camera, lenses, soap, and so on during the day. And these can't all be stored in pockets. (Note that this stipulation is for touring bags. If you don't plan to have anything on your rack that will impair entry, don't worry about it. However, you will be able to locate items in front-loading bags far more easily than in top-loaders, even when the bags are off the bike.)

Other things I prefer in saddlebags:

External pockets. I find these very convenient for items I use often. One of the finest panniers made is nearly pocketless (a very handy mesh pouch exists), and I've had fine tours with it. Internal pockets are present, and I added to these by putting some of my smaller things in stuff sacks of different colors. However, *if all other things were equal* I would opt for external pockets.

External mesh pockets. I am almost always drying clothes somewhere on my bike. Mesh pockets make this unembarrassing; I don't like traveling through towns with my socks and underwear in plain sight.

Zipper entry. Side-release buckles on straps are quick, but zippers are more convenient. (You'll find buckles primarily on bags for ATBs, discussed later.)

Easy attachment/removal. My hands are large. I therefore find some (but only some) of the behind-the-bag attachment systems difficult, if they require anything to be grabbed or pulled. Most systems have a simple metal S-hook to attach beneath the rack support arm; the bag is then lifted up until the top hooks are over the top of the rack. Quick and easy.

Mountain-bike bags require a greater grip, and some ingenious methods have been developed. But for most tourers, the simple hook-and-spring/tension-strap combination is sufficient to keep the bag from jumping off the rack.

However, this does not mean that the bag will stay snugged against the rack support arms. If the bottom tension strap or spring weakens, the bag will move away from the bike during bumps or while leaning into turns, then bang back into position. Such lateral sway in the rear will be felt by the rider, will weaken fabric and hardware stress points in the bag, and might, over time, cause a rack's mounting bolts to work loose.

Decreased lateral sway is a selling point for the slightly more difficult to mount behind-the-bag attachment systems. The tension-strap crowd has responded with some excellent, close-tolerance springs and straps designed not to stretch, and additional compression straps to hold the load in place against the bike when in rough terrain. With the tough, unbreakable back stiffeners contributing to the bag's overall rigidity, I have found no problem of sway with the better tension-strap packs.

Rain covers. Heavy-weight Cordura bags, especially when backed with a urethane or other kind of waterproofing and equipped with wide zipper covers, provide fairly good protection against the elements. But come a heavy storm and it's a different story. You will be dry, if you've gotten into poncho and chaps or a full rain suit before the world turned wet. Your belongings, however, will be soaked.

The answer to storms for some people is to duck for cover at first cloud. But you'll miss far more than you know. It might look miserable—a yellow-ponchoed cyclist moving through the rain—but it isn't, if you're prepared. Know how it feels to sit next to a fire, warm and dry, while outside the window a winter tempest howls? Well, it's the same thing here. Only better, because you can feel and *smell* the storm.

Pannier rain covers—the best way to handle inclement weather.

You'll enjoy it more, of course, if you know your gear is dry. (You'll also enjoy the ride more because you'll be *lighter*, as wet bags and belongings add an unbelievable amount of water weight and take a long time to dry out.) Rain covers—*completely* waterproof—are the answer. If you have bought them from the same company that put out your panniers, they should fit snugly. Nevertheless, long before the ride, make sure that they will slip on over a *fully* loaded pannier.

Most are made of a urethane-coated nylon taffeta and look like a giant yellow shower cap. (Some studies have shown yellow to be best for visibility in the rain.) These thin, lightweight covers take up little room when off the bags, and are well worth their cost. Be sure the covers come equipped with a grommeted drain hole in the bottom, to let out the moisture that sneaks inside by flying off the wheels onto the uncovered back portion of the pannier. Alternatives of trash bags *inside* one's panniers, or packing all belongings in separate ziplock bags, will be discussed in a later chapter. I'll mention now, however, that my strong preference is for rain covers.

Large zipper tabs. Removing heavy winter or lightweight long-finger gloves (worn often during even summer tours, when mornings can be chilly) to grasp a zipper soon becomes a bother. I therefore like large tabs. Double zippers—two "slides" on a single zipper closing—are also convenient. But I don't like the noise of all these metal zipper tabs clanging around when I'm in the saddle. One answer I've found is to wrap the tab with a rubber band; a buddy of mine coats his with a kind of rubber cement.

Some final words on panniers. Think of what you'll be taking on your ride, and buy with size requirements in mind. One nice way of starting out (while you're still smarting from the cost of the bike) is to buy front panniers only. For weekend rides or motel trips you can get by with this capacity, then add a front rack and large rear panniers when you take off on longer tours.

I am continually asked what brand of bag I use on tour, and though I hesitate in most instances to give specific names I will provide it here. For my around-town commuting and short weekend tours I find most bags to be sufficient. But my preference on long rides, when I am carrying a lot and must count on durability, is the combination of Bruce Gordon racks and Robert Beckman Designs (formerly Needle Works) panniers. This is not to say other brands haven't worked for me on the road. But as I must carry some twenty-five pounds of camera gear, in addition to my normal touring load, these state-of-the-art racks and packs are my personal choice.

Handlebar Bags

I don't ride without one. Who wants to stop each time you look at the map? Or get off the bike to grab a snack? Besides, where's a better place to carry a camera, and the little personal items of toothbrush/paste, pen, postcards, and the like, which you'll want with you inside the tent at night or in cafés? The best of handlebar bags are easily removed, and when equipped with a shoulder strap become the perfect companion bag—on *and* off the bike.

Taking pictures from the bike is also made simple by the "camera inserts" available from some pack companies. These sturdy, padded foam inserts drop into a large handlebar bag, providing a safe-riding cushion for camera and lens. (Some come with moveable dividers so that a rider can custom-fit his photography gear.) I pack my heavy 35mm camera here, with a large zoom lens attached, plus cleaning fluid and paper, brush, a polarized filter, and several rolls of film. In this way when a bear appears, or a quickly moving cloudbank, I simply jump out of the saddle and grab my camera—all while straddling the bike.

HOWEVER, what's the sense of having all this great gear at your fingertips if it's going to get soaked? The simple answer is to develop a rain cover, but at this writing I know of only one company (Lone Peak) that offers covers for bar bags. That doesn't mean there aren't more available when you read this, or that I haven't somehow missed a new addition to the fold.

The "engineer" cyclists will be wincing at the thought of all this weight so high off the ground. We've talked already of the need to keep weight as low as possible, thereby lowering one's center of gravity and gaining a more stable ride. Once again we are at the point of trade-offs. Buy a high-quality, well-suspended bar bag and you'll find that you can carry a fair load.

Suggestions for your search (in addition to the general remarks above, such as starting early, taking your time . . .):

—Buy a handlebar bag with a map case if you'll ever be far from home, and make sure the map case is large enough for a folded map.

—If you plan to carry camera gear, pay even greater attention to the suspension system; take your things to a bike shop, load up a bag, and try it out; it is understandable that a salesman might at first balk at this, but *you're* the one who might be dropping fifty bucks.

—Look for shoulder-strap/rain-cover/quality of materials and stitching.

Seat Bags

These are the little "wedge" packs that fit up under the saddle. You are probably thinking that if they fit under the saddle they should be called "saddlebags," but when they first came out, years ago, they were marketed under the name of seat bags, and the name stuck. But the greater problem is the mental image that pops into most Americans' heads when the term "saddlebag" is heard. Don't you think of dusty, sweat-stained leather bags hanging down on either side of the horse and filled with beef jerky and extra bullets? Of course you do. And it would be a crime to take a history-filled word like saddlebags and apply it, today, to some wimpy little pouch.

Besides, panniers (an extremely *un*-American term that has always rankled me) look like saddlebags, and bike riders pack them around just as horse riders did—mounted and unmounted alike. Another point: Who has ever heard of a "saddle post"? No one, of course, and it is to this seatpost that a portion of the seat bag attaches. Most riders call their saddles "seats" anyway.

Back to seat bags. I prefer the ones that:

—are made of heavy Cordura to provide inherent stability;

—have an attachment system that allows the bag to be snugged up under the saddle, rather than hang down from it;

—are of sufficient size for my poncho and chaps (the perfect quick-access spot for these items);

—have a stripe of reflective tape rather than a heavy reflector.

Toe Covers

These little beauties fit over the toeclips, shielding the front of the foot from rain and wind. I don't use them in warm weather (I want the airflow then, and my large waterproof shoe covers keep the foot dry anyway), but they're great to help keep toes warm in the cold.

Rack Packs/Rack Duffles

I don't use these on tour, for they fit on the rear rack occupied by my house and bed (tent and sleeping bag). And on a one-day or motel tour I usually prefer the weight lower, in panniers.

Duffles are pretty good for commuting, however, and the "insulated" rack packs keep summertime beverages cool. Relatively new to the market is a dandy hard-shell (bright ABS plastic) "duffle" that mounts to the rack top in such a way as to make theft extremely time-consuming. This waterproof "Vetta Box" has 270 cubic inches of storage, and a hinged lid that locks shut with a key. Extremely lightweight, there is space beneath it for a U-lock. I find it very handy for around-town use, and mention it here for those who feel they can fit inside it all they'll need for a one-day ride.

On-person Bags

I swore after my first cross-country ride with a backpack that I would never tour again with something clinging to my body. This is still true. However, I feel the need to suggest two kinds of bags for commuters and one- or two-day cyclists who wish to begin their training before they can purchase racks and packs, or who wish to keep their bikes "clean" of such accoutrements but still need storage space.

The first of these alternatives is the waist or "fanny" pack. I find them so comfortable that I can almost forget them as I ride. Several manufacturers put out excellent waist packs, so I won't bother giving names, but be sure to search for one with the capacity you'll require (they've been getting larger in recent years). I also find that those made of heavier fabrics, and which distribute the contents up and down my back a bit—as opposed to out (away) from my waist—feel better during the ride.

The problem with waist packs when commuting, however, is that many of us need to lug around papers, books, notebooks, and legal pads, and yet will not put up with the wet shirt that comes from pedaling with a backpack. The cavalry has arrived, and, oddly enough, from New York. An innovative entrepreneur (and former Manhattan bike messenger) named Paul Rosenfeld eyeballed the need for this two-wheeled carrying capacity and developed the

Paul's Cycle Sac.

"Cycle Sac" shoulder bag. Actually, that should be Sacs (with an "s"), for there are now both thin-tire and mountain-bike models. The former is a classic beauty of heavy canvas, a rubberized waterproof inner-coating (I even trust my slides to it during a storm), a size sufficient for small art portfolios, and a small-of-the-back-hugging, out-of-the-way-when-pedaling design. Perfect for the college crowd, it also lets the rest of us remain on two wheels even when the load for the office is large.

The ATB model is just a bit smaller, far lighter, constructed of waterproofed cordura, and is equipped with side-release Fastex buckles and a second strap that snaps across the torso and holds the bag against you as you beat the trails or curbs. (Address and toll-free number are in Appendix.)

Rack Straps

Once again we have a problem with terminology. If you don't know what is being referred to by rack straps, think "bungees." (Ugh—what a word!)

It has always amazed me that some cyclists will spend a great deal of money shaving grams from components, and then add ounces elsewhere without a thought. This is exactly the case when it comes to rack straps. Lift three or four of the regular kind—those with large metal hooks on either end of half-inch elastic bands—and you'll have the weight of a rear derailleur. And although I am not so concerned about weight as many tourers, I don't *prefer* packing around more tonnage than a ride requires.

An alternative to the commonplace has been provided by Lone Peak, through what is called "BH-36 Adjustable Bungee Hooks." Take time to look to these, or at the Blackburn elastic strap (nonadjustable; attaches in the wrong way for my gear), or at others like them, when more companies see the need and move to fill it. Lone Peak's straps are one-quarter-inch rubber, enclosed in nylon and ending in tough, lightweight plastic hooks. They are even made to be "personalized"—cut to whatever length your personal touring load requires.

Bike Carts

I met a woman one evening while pedaling through a small Colorado town, and asked her if she knew of a campground nearby. There wasn't one, but after a few minutes' conversation she gave me her husband's name and directions to her house, and suggested I spend the night with them. It is a surprisingly common occurrence when on tour, but I had in this instance stumbled upon two strangers who were also accomplished cross-country cyclists.

An around-town and on-tour alternative to panniers—the CycleTote Trailer.

Their method of touring, however, was unique. No panniers were used, just handlebar bags and—behind the man's bike—a trailer. He was far stronger, the wife told me with a smile, and this discrepancy in load thus evened out their pace.

My own experience with bike carts began when I was living car-less, and bought a relatively inexpensive "byKart" to transport all those items too large to fit into packs. Constructed entirely of a heavy metal and equipped with very small, solid-rubber tires, it nevertheless performed flawlessly when called upon to carry home a months' supply of groceries.

I next acquired a very different model made for touring, and used in on many rides. This was the CycleTote "Tour" model, a light, weather-tight cart with eight thousand cubic inches of space, a welded, tubular aluminum frame, and a "No Roll" safety hitch. Equipped with two 27″ bicycle wheels, the trailer was sized to fit easily through the standard doorway. (This feature made it excellent for pulling into town, wheeling the cart into a motel room, releasing it, and then riding about completely unencumbered.) It tracked nicely behind my bike, and I still use it on occasion. But my personal preference is still panniers.

If you and a touring friend or spouse have greatly different riding speeds you might consider such a trailer. And if you have children you should give carts even greater thought. When the kids are small they can ride in a behind-the-saddle position in any number of "child carriers" (one well-made model is the Troxel Highback), but remember the problems of having too much weight up high on a bike. I suggest a helmet for little ones when in such seats, and serious consideration of the CycleTote child model, the Cannondale "Bugger," the Burley trailer, or others for taking a child on tour. Most are equipped with weatherproof canopies and wheel shields to keep the youngster's fingers away from spokes. (Cannondale, Burley, and Troxel products are often found in bike shops, but you must write to CycleTote and byKart for information. Addresses are in Appendix.)

SPARE PARTS AND TOOLS

Tire

You will recall that in Chapter 1 I talked about carrying a spare tire on long tours. I mentioned both "foldable" clinchers—the newer kind, which take up little room and therefore can be carried inside one's panniers—and regular tires, which must be "figure-eighted" for safe packing. Good luck with the following:

Begin by holding the tire before you, with hands at the three o'clock and nine o'clock positions. Now bring your hands together, toward your chest. You can see that two long, narrow ovals have been created, one above and one below your hands.

Next, take hold of both sides of the tire with your left hand, and with your right reach through the lower loop toward the upper loop. Take hold of the upper and pull it down toward your left hand (which is still holding both sides of the tire).

As you bring this upper loop downward you'll notice that you have created two more loops—smaller ones, this time. Gradually release the grip of your left hand and use it to fold these smaller loops upon one another. You have produced four small circles of tire, all with the metal bead intact. Use tape or light rope to keep it from springing back into its original shape.

Folding the tire—Step 1.   *Step 2.*

Step 3.

Step 4.

Step 5.

Tube

I pack a single spare tube, and throw it quickly into my tire when a puncture appears. (That is, *after* checking the tire for whatever thorn or piece of glass that made the original hole.) This allows me to repair the tube in camp that night or at my leisure.

Oil

Subject a chain to rain and snow on tour without occasional lubrication and it will, after time, tell you about it. The squeaking is unbearable, as is the rough shifting you'll endure if you aren't good to your derailleurs. But how to carry oil? Any metal can is far too heavy; plastic bottles always seem to leak.

I was overjoyed when one company came out with a pencil-thin, syringe-looking plastic container, which allowed for the application of individual drops of oil and weighed not much at all. Unfortunately, I found over time that this plastic container was like all the rest. It cracked, and spilled its greasy contents on everything in my tool bag.

My solution is to carry my oil in a hard plastic 35mm film cannister. (Film removed.) This I place inside a small ziplock bag, along with a tiny plastic eye-dropper. I've never had a film cannister open up on me, and the eyedropper allows for judicious and precise oil use.

Grease

Take some along, just in case you have to repack a wheel. There's no need, however, to lug a big tube. Your bike shop will probably carry these large tubes of green, water-resistant Phil Wood grease. It's excellent, but messy. Squeeze it out into another 35mm film cannister, making it about three-quarters full. That should be plenty.

Since we're up to two film cannisters already, with more soon to come, I should mention marking them. I've tried all sorts of "permanent" pens, but found them inadequate. I therefore write the contents of my film containers in small letters on the clear side of a 3 × 5 card, cut around the words, and with a long piece of clear tape (wide enough to enclose the tiny bit of card completely) apply it to the film cannister side. I use a long piece of tape so as to wrap one end over the other, thus ensuring its permanent position.

Air Gauge

Yes, I use a gas-station air hose every chance I get. But I *never* trust their hose-attached gauges. I couldn't afford the blown tires.

Pack along any good air gauge, and even the heavier ones will be worth their weight.

Brake Cable/Gear Cable

Most of these are so well made today that you'll go years without needing a replacement. But take along one of each anyway. And keep the little "cable ends" in place (crimped onto the cut, free end of every cable), to avoid fraying.

Brake Pad

I pack a couple of these on very long tours only—just the pads, not the metal shoes they slip into.

Chain Links

Only once in all my touring have I needed a spare chain link to replace a broken one. The recent-generation chains are of such close tolerances that they hold up longer than the ones I rode with back in the sixties. I now pack three spare links.

Spokes

I carry five extra spokes, taped to my left chainstay. Each stainless-steel head (or "nipple") is individually taped to its spoke, to prevent road vibration from backing it off.

Chances are, you will never break a spoke if you load and ride properly. And if you do snap one, it will be on the freewheel ("dished") side of the rear wheel. "Dishing" refers to the way in which spokes on that side must come from the rim to the hub at a sharper angle, due to axle space taken up by the freewheel. Unfortunately, this demands removal of the freewheel—the single greatest problem (aside from food poisoning in Cairo, dysentery in India, and finding my old Ranger camp in 'Nam) of my around-the-world ride. However, some wizard has come up with a wonderful "pocket vise" removal tool, which you'll meet shortly.

Bearings

Bearing sizes generally fall into these categories:

$\frac{3}{16}''$—front hub
$\frac{1}{4}''$—rear hub, bottom bracket
$\frac{1}{8}''$—freewheel
$\frac{5}{32}''$—pedal, headset

Ask the salesman, or find out yourself, what size bearings your bike has. Carry three or four of each (except for the freewheel size) if you're planning a very long tour. In this manner you can replace a pitted or cracked bearing, or one that gets lost during repacking.

Rack Mounting Bolts

I take on all tours two replacement rack bolts, as discussed earlier.

Before you get concerned at the length of the following tool list, understand that most riders do not carry many tools at all. I'll provide comments later on as to which ones may be left at home when you take just short trips.

Crescent Wrench

Six-inch adjustable.

Screwdriver

Regular (flat) blade, blade tip $\frac{3}{16}''$ wide, overall length six inches.

Channel Locks

Seven-inch.

Tire Levers

I carry two rather heavy ones, primarily because their decades of service and retention of quality justify—to me—the weight. An ounce or more could be saved were I to turn to the newer alloy or nonmetal types, but I'd feel guilty leaving my old ones at home. If you prefer metal and opt for the lightweight alloy ones, be sure to buy quality. Inspect them closely, as cheap levers will bend. Some of the poor ones also have sharp edges that can put holes in your tube, and aren't of sufficient length to grip both spoke and tire securely at the same time. (Explanation of all this is in *Repairs*.)

Allen Wrenches

It is essential, first, that you pack along a wrench of the proper size for each allen-head bolt on your bike, and, second, that you do not lose them on the trail.

Cone Wrenches

Don't pack on tour the ones designed for shop use. These are pretty, last forever, and sport bright blue plastic handles for a sure grip. But they are also far heavier than necessary. I carry two alloy cone wrenches, one sized for thirteen and fourteen millimeters, the other for fifteen and sixteen millimeters. Be sure to check your cone sizes before buying. (Don't worry if you haven't a clue about what a cone is at this time, much less how to use a wrench on them. You'll learn it in *Repairs*.)

Chain Rivet Tool

Necessary to replace a link, repair a frozen one.

Spoke Nipple Wrench

Used to adjust spoke tension.

Freewheel Tool

There are several different kinds of these tools, so make sure you're buying the right one. Your specifications chart or salesman will be able to tell you, or you can remove your rear wheel and read the name on the freewheel core. One side of the tool fits into the freewheel; the other side is beveled flat, to be held fast in a vise or huge crescent wrench.

Pocket Vise

This is the ingenious creation which, when used in conjunction with the freewheel tool above, allows a rider to remove his freewheel on the road. Seven times on my world ride I'd have given almost anything to have this.

Cotterless Crank-Removal Tool

Once more, you must make sure you're buying the right one for your particular crank.

Adjustable Cup Tool

I have never carried on the road the heavy tool I use at home to work on the adjustable cup side of my bottom bracket. My screwdriver tip serves imperfectly in budging the cup (thereby adjusting the pressure against the bearings), but it serves. (I have never been forced to repack bottom bracket bearings while on tour, being sure to begin long rides with good bearings and fresh grease. I therefore do not carry the very heavy lock ring/fixed cup bottom bracket tool. With the great number of sealed bearings today I will be even more surprised if you should ever run into difficulty on tour.)

Bike Locks

Bicycle security is of course of paramount importance while on tour. Losing a bike to thieves when at home is no fun either, but if you're ever stranded on the trail you'll quickly understand why horse-stealing in the Old West brought the offender to the smoking end of a six-shooter, or a lasting, impressionable encounter with a rope.

But how do you go about protecting not only your rig but all the gear piled on it? The best bike locks—those U-shaped beauties marketed under the names of Citadel, Kryptonite, and others—weigh far too much (about two pounds) for the road. And even then you stand to lose everything but the frame.

I have, however, been extremely fortunate in having never lost a single item to theft while on tour. And this is true even though I most often pack no lock whatsoever. (When I have carried one it was usually a short, thin cable and lightweight key-operated lock.) Why have I been so fortunate? The answer lies in realizing that most such thefts are "casual" in nature, and then working to ensure that the thief must take a greater degree of risk than most such casual criminals will venture.

For instance, all my pannier pockets—even empty ones—are zipped closed when I'm away from my bike. (If I am particularly concerned I also slip on my rain covers.) I choose cafés and a table inside where I can see my bike, and if this is impossible I search for a nearby gas station or house with a fenced yard or wide porch and ask if they would mind watching my rig for an hour. On weekend rides, when I expect to be pedaling around a particular town quite a bit, I'll sometimes pack a heavy U-lock; on longer tours, when my load prohibits such additional weight, I leave my bike in a motel room, with a campground manager, or at a garage or police/fire station. I have found that people identify immediately with a tourer's fear of loss, and respond accordingly.

Here are two additional points concerning leaving a bike within view outside a café. First, you do not endear yourself with the manager if you lean your mount against the window; find some other means of support. Second, guard against making it easy for someone to push your bike away. Hook the end of a shock cord (bungie) around a spoke, preferably behind a pannier. In this manner the thief cannot easily locate the problem, and will probably give up the attempt.

Remember that most bike thefts are of clean, unencumbered machines, and that very few people could simply hop aboard a heavily loaded bike and pedal off before you could reach them. Most losses will therefore be of items in one's bags, and here you can foil even those smarter thieves who know we like to keep valuables in handlebar packs. Be sure, when purchasing your bag, that it is easily removed, and then take it with you whenever you leave the bike. Or keep those items you value most in a small stuff sack inside your handlebar pack, and carry at least this with you when you're in stores and cafés.

When camped, I once again dally a shock-cord end around a spoke, to slow down the culprit if he attempts a theft at night. If I am at a busy campground near or in a town, I go one step farther. I lay my bike on the ground next to my tent and hook a second shock cord from it to one of the tent guy lines. Like a fish jerking a rod tip, the thief's movements would alert me that something was up.

Remember too that it has been necessary throughout history to protect one's belongings; those who make themselves miserable over the supposed loss of the moral, upright "good old days" have not cycle-toured through towns whose people opened doors and hearts to two-wheeled strangers. Naturally, we must take precautions against the few. But the real crime lies in letting then engender a distrustful view of the world at large.

A shock-cord end round a spoke will slow down the "casual" thief.

3

Equipment for
the Biker

FOLLOW THE ADVICE in the first two chapters and your mobility is assured; the bike is ready for the road. Now we turn our attention to the *biker,* to the clothing and camping gear necessary for you to ride comfortably, stay well, and sleep bug-free and dry.

CLOTHING

Comfort and durability are two obvious qualities required in clothing for the tour. Less obvious are color (to be seen by motorists, and to look good in slides), age (begin a trip with brand new clothes and you're likely to be unhappily surprised at shrinkage), and the ability to be machine-washed and dried together. Sleeves and tails of shirts and jackets must be long enough to cover the upper torso when stretched out in riding position; the legs of long pants and long-legged underwear must likewise be capable of reaching the ankles when pedaling.

Finally, clothing should be chosen with "layering" in mind. That is, with only a pannier-full of options the biker must be able to adapt to all climates met along the trail, and to the body temperature variations brought on by intense exercise. A heavy, bulky sweater or coat might feel great when first leaving the tent in cool weather, but you'll be cursing it at your first hill. The answer is

Yours truly on a solo, off-road winter tour.

layers of clothing, which, when combined in different fashions, will keep you comfortable whatever the weather or physical strain.

What follows is the clothing I pack on long rides, in regions of great elevation diversity and/or at times when the weather might change quickly—such as at my favorite touring seasons of fall through spring. Naturally, you will modify this list to your own body preferences, and tailor it even more depending upon length and season of ride. But let me leave you with this thought before we begin the particulars—a personal motto, if you will, that applies to the whole of packing for a trip: "Go prepared for anything, and then enjoy it all." You've already freed yourself from the shackles of motorized, regimented vacations through your choice of cycle touring. Now free yourself from the blue-sky-only mentality by packing wisely (and a bit more heavily, perhaps, than you'd prefer) when it comes to clothes and camping gear.

Clothing for General Use

T-shirts (3). Bright colors, preferably yellow for desert hot-weather rides, loose-fitting in trunk and sleeves to allow airflow if desired; I like a breast pocket for pen, and a high neck.

Long-sleeved shirt (1). No, I don't wear bike jerseys. I don't like the tight fit, the feel of the material, or the uniformlike instant identification as a biker when the crazy colored bands are seen. My preference is something along the lines of a Patagonia sweatshirt—a soft pullover, single color, a two- or three-snap neck that is sufficiently warm when closed and airy when open. Once again I want to feel like a traveler, not just a biker, when on tour but off the bike. The arguments that a jersey's material and tight fit provide less wind resistance seem not only terribly minor, but a consideration with which tourers shouldn't have to contend. And the great attribute of pockets across the back? I can see it with a racer on a training ride, since he's removed pockets from where they ought to be—in one's shorts. But tourers have handlebar bags for bananas and hats and gloves, and pockets in their shorts for bandanas, a comb, and a knife.

Riding shorts (2). Some books can't say enough about the use of racing shorts for touring. They go on and on about how the tight-fitting, mid-thigh cut is necessary to prevent the legs from moving up and chafing the skin, that the lack of seams/chamois insert/no need for underwear make for the most comfortable ride. I mention these points so you'll know to give them a try. But my bet is that unless speed is your primary goal you'll opt for something practical (and less humorous) even when you aren't pedaling.

First, the all-black color makes them feel hot on me, aided in this by the fact that no air can get past the long, tight-fitting legs. There are no pockets. The chamois insert may feel nice, but it requires care; one author suggests he prefers to "wash the shorts in warm water with a mild soap, rinse well, shape the chamois before drying, work it soft by hand after drying, and apply baby oil after every few washings"! As to the point of racing shorts doing away with the need for undershorts, I don't agree. I prefer to don fresh undershorts daily, but can get several days out of a pair of riding shorts. And about the seams being such a bother? Either I've gotten used to it, or the fact that I'm not locked into the saddle like a Tour de France rider keeps it from bothering me.

A few companies have realized, finally, that racers and tourers aren't identical in need and preference. "Touring shorts" are now available, usually (and unfortunately) with "cargo" pockets on either thigh—guaranteed to empty their contents whenever you are doing anything but pedaling. (If you have the same problem, you might sew a strip of velcro under either flap.)

But by far the best shorts around, in my opinion, are those made by Sportif USA. I don't like to plug one manufacturer over another, but in some cases I think it necessary, so that at least you'll know one brand to check out before making your *own* selection. I buy the ones that are khaki in color (thereby going well with any colored shirt or T-shirt I might wear), made of an extremely durable blend of polyester/cotton/spandex (the last material allowing the shorts to stretch comfortably in all directions), with zippered back pockets, two deep front pockets, two lower-front button-down patch pockets, and a small watch pocket as well, wide belt loops, YKK zipper in front, and all stress seams double-stitched.

Belt (1). Web, zippered, compartment for money, hard plastic adjustable buckle; this style is light in weight, good for adjusting to your slimmer figure (noticeable after even a short time on tour), great for keeping larger bills always close by, and capable of being used as an emergency sling.

Undershorts (3). As with T-shirts, I carry three so that I always have a clean pair in reserve, a fresh pair on, and the pair I hand-washed the night before drying in the mesh portion of my saddlebag.

Long pants (1). I'm still not satisfied in this department. By far the best option would be a pair of above-the-knee leggings that connect by zipper to one's touring shorts. (A small flap could hide the zipper). But such complicated construction is beyond my talents in sewing, and the single pair I've seen for sale were far beyond my budget. (These were also of 100 percent cotton, and would have worn out in the seat.)

My answer therefore is to pack a relatively lightweight pair of "hiking pants," made of material similar to the shorts described above. When rolled carefully they take up little room in a pannier, and still look nice when worn about town.

After writing the two preceding paragraphs I took a tough, four-day/four-mountain-pass ATB tour in the San Juan Range of southwest Colorado. One of my fellow riders had along a pair of Patagonia Featherweight Shell Pants, and though I've not yet tried them out myself I think they might just be the solution to this difficult problem. Weighing only seven ounces, they are water-resistant, breathable, made of ripstop nylon, have two zipper diagonal vents to allow access to the pockets of one's shorts underneath, sport an elasticized waistband, and can be crammed into even the most well-stuffed pannier. Unfortunately, they come only in red and electric blue, but the latter is not so conspicuous as the name implies.

Gym shorts (1). Many motel and city pools have restrictions against wearing regular shorts into the water, and thus a pair of gym shorts comes in handy. These can also be worn as a pair of riding shorts in a pinch.

Insulated underwear (1 pair). We've come a long way since the long-john days of thick cotton. They felt good until hard work occurred, when perspiration soaked the fabric and remained—wet and clammy—next to the skin. Stop working for a bit while still outside, and a chill was inevitable.

Until just a year ago I suggested polypropylene underwear for its "wicking" abilities—the movement of perspiration away from the skin and surrounding fabric to the next garment worn. This did away with clamminess, but at a price of slightly greater retention of body odor, prohibitions against machine-drying, and a loss of softness over time. However, I found the wicking extremely beneficial, that polypro dried very quickly by itself, and that with the use of fabric softener I could keep the garments relatively supple.

And then came capilene. Same wicking principal, but none of the polypro drawbacks. As with polypro, capilene comes in expedition, midweight, and lightweight thicknesses. My choice is midweight, for warmth even when sitting around a campfire (and when my sleeping bag needs help in keeping me warm), and any color but white. In this way I can, if necessary, wear the top as an outer shirt in public and have it pass for a sweatshirt. I also suggest a two-piece, top-and-bottom set, rather than a union suit. Not only do I find this far more comfortable when cycling, but sometimes I want more insulation on top, but not on my legs.

Leggings (1). What does a cyclist do when the morning chill requires covering the legs for that first half-hour of riding? If long pants are worn he must find some place to change into shorts, a difficulty when in urban areas or near a busy road. And what of the days when mountains are encountered, bringing on tough, warm climbs to summits and cold descents?

My answer for many years has been the washable wool leggings put out by Protogs. These provide just the necessary amount of warmth, yet can be rolled down and cuffed about the ankles in an instant, and removed altogether without having to hide behind a bush.

Socks (3 pairs). My choice for all but midwinter touring is thick, white cotton/polypropylene/nylon blends. They are a bit hotter than thin socks would be, but I prefer the cushioned feeling of a thicker layer between my foot and my shoe. All-cotton socks aren't sufficiently durable for me, a problem that I have with all-wool models as well. I therefore choose a wool/poly/nylon blend for winter, sometimes with a capilene liner for extra warmth and to wick moisture away from the foot. Three pairs are packed for the same reason as with underwear—one being worn, one drying, a clean pair in reserve for the next day. (If I'm unable to wash these out, as is the case in deserts when water is too scarce, the thicker materials maintain their cushion better than the cooler, thinner kinds.)

Riding shoes (1 pair). No matter which shoe you finally choose for the road, it must have a very stiff sole. Years ago it was difficult to find anything sufficiently stiff between the extremes of the lightweight, black Italian racing shoes, and heavy construction boots. In fact, when my buddy and I at last reached the California coast during the "worlder" and determined that we'd try to make a winter Rockies crossing, we decided upon the high-top army air-borne "jump" boots for the trip.

I tried the racing shoes one year, on a hot-weather ride from Salt Lake to Yellowstone. Not only were they uncomfortable, with their extremely thin but rock-hard sole and unpadded upper, but their slick bottom made walking difficult on anything but sidewalks. Some tourers, I am told, not only wear these racing shoes, but ride with cleats attached. (Cleats are affixed permanently to the bottom of racing shoes, and are designed to lock the foot onto the pedal for greater efficiency.) They either clop about town on these cleats, which make one's heels stand lower than the ball of the foot, or are constantly changing shoes whenever leaving the bike. Now, I've read that this is done, but I've never seen it. The only person I know personally who tried changing shoes constantly did it for only one ride. In theory the practice makes some sense, given the greater speed and pedal "feel" that come from being locked to the pedal. (People who use cleats reach down and pull their straps tight each time they climb back in the saddle, and must learn to release them in a split second when trouble looms. I keep mine very loose, for easy, carefree foot removal.) And how long can it take to slip on a second pair of shoes?

But think of it a minute. How many times a day do you think you'd be changing shoes? Besides, racing shoes lace up, as no doubt your second pair of shoes would as well, if you planned to do anything but shuffle about town in them. So now you add the time of two changes and two lacings and unlacings *each* time you stop. And what if it's raining? Do you really want both pairs of shoes wet? And how about removing the pannier raincover, and opening the bag in the rain to find the second pair? Finally, add the weight of the second pair of shoes to your overall load. Is this efficiency? I keep reading articles and books suggesting just such a plan for footwear, and each time I shake my head and wonder if these folks ever really tour at all. A weekender, perhaps, or a week-long ride where mileage is a primary concern. But to me this all sounds like very troublesome travel.

The first bicycle industry "touring shoe" that I recall was the "Bata Biker"—a low-cut tennis shoe in style, black with colored bands, and a tiny little heel that once again made one feel as if earth shoes were being worn. Granted, they were stiff. And light in weight. But I always had the feeling that if I wished real hard and clicked them twice I wouldn't have to pedal home. Besides, who wants to walk into a bar at the end of a hard day looking like Peter Pan?

Finally, someone in the industry (who actually *tours* instead of just training) realized the problem and developed alternatives. I had already left the biking world to find solutions in the excellent lightweight hiking boots made by Nike (the low-cut model Thunderdome and its predecessors for warm-weather thin-tire and mountain-bike touring; the high-top Zealand for cold ATB rides), and several models of the less expensive Hi-Tec brand. My personal preference after testing these (and the extremely lightweight Lake and unbelievably stiff Puma II brands) is still the costly Nike models mentioned above. Granted, the Thunderdome and New Zealand Nikes are not designed for cycling, as are some of their other models (and the Hi-Tecs, Lakes, and Pumas I've tried). But I find their greater weight is, for me, offset by the lasting comfort (on and off the bike), overall performance, and apparent indestructibility.

Most of my fellow tourers prefer the Nike and other brand bike shoes of mesh/nylon uppers, nylon/fiberglass plates for stiffness, and hard rubber outsoles. So shop around, pay close attention to construction, and choose carefully.

A couple of final warnings: first, although I once did a three-thousand-mile ride (along the Lewis and Clark Trail) in a pair of rather stiff jogging shoes, I suggest you avoid such footwear unless you add the Spenco orthotics, which are available at many bike shops.) These can be inserted into any shoe to make it sufficiently stiff for cycling. (Remember, however, that a well-formed upper with extra padding at toeclip and strap contact points is also a necessity for comfort.) Second, "clipless" pedals—those that lock the foot onto the pedal without the use of clips and straps—have the same drawbacks as cleats. Don't underestimate the hassle of changing shoes each time you leave the bike.

Camp moccasins (1 pair). The all-leather, no-additional-sole kind. Light in weight and taking up almost no room in a pannier, moccasins are the perfect evening footwear around camp or motel room. My feet appreciate the comfort; my daytime shoes have a chance to air out or dry.

Bandanas (2). You'll quickly find out why these were a cowboy staple in the West. Their uses are too numerous to list, but at least you won't require handkerchiefs on the trail when these are around.

Riding gloves (1 pair). The purpose of this clothing article is protection of the hands against the nerve-damaging pressure exerted when leaning toward the handlebars all day, protection of the palms in case of a fall, and the comfort gained through a bit of padding between your skin and the bars. They are usually made of a leather covering on the palm, with sorbothane or other padding beneath it, leather half-fingers, and a fabric net or mesh over the back of the hand, to hold the glove together and yet not be too warm.

I like the feel of these in cool weather, but switch to Spenco "palm pads" for rough, dirt road hot-weather riding, and no gloves at all when it's hot and I'm on a pavement-only tour. This is made possible because of the thick leather wrapping around my bars, and the fact that I tilt up and raise my handlebars sufficiently to end some of the pressure exerted by the forward lean.

Riding cap (1). When it's warm I wear a baseball cap, for the practical reasons of a large bill to shade the face (I turn the bill around during fast decents, to keep the hat from blowing off), and the cooling effect of a shaded air chamber above the head. But most of the time when cycling I employ a cap that goes by several different names, and is therefore best described. Think of the dapper caps worn by drivers of foreign sports cars, when the tops are down. Usually they have a snap above the slight bill, and are aerodynamically shaped to handle the wind—by sloping downward in front.

I find that such a cap, if it fits rather tight, will remain on my head despite passing trucks and headwinds. The shape is also an advantage in removing it while pedaling, yet keeping it nearby; I simply slip the bill into the back of my pants, where it rides until I need it again. Just a year ago I found the *perfect* cap of this variety, made by a fellow in Salt Lake. It is called the "Roly" after its creator Roly Pearson. I had thought before I met him that the name originated from the cap's ability to be rolled up without damage. There are models made of lightweight wool or of nearly weightless silk, and both fit nicely beneath helmets for cold-weather riding. They have no snap in front or hard cardboard bill (meaning I don't have to remove the cap when taking photographs, for the bill acts simply as a cushion for the camera as it folds against my forehead, and it is a welcome insulator against the cold metal camera body in winter), and earflaps inside, which may look dopey when worn, but are welcome in a pinch. (Address in Appendix.)

Foul and Cold-Weather Gear

Boots (1 pair). These take the place of the riding shoes discussed above. My choice is usually an over-the-ankle lightweight boot. In less than arctic conditions I ride with something similar to those described earlier (counting on heavy socks and toeclip toe covers to ward off frostbite); on long winter tours I use an old pair of fleece-insulated ski touring boots. I had the extended sole in front ground off by a cobbler, inserted my Spenco orthotics, and rode warm through a Midwest December.

Rain boots (1 pair). This is, without a doubt, the greatest problem for me on tour. I have tried every possible combination of available products and still have not found a covering that (1) keeps my feet completely dry, (2) will not rip when in contact with rattrap (thin-tire) or bear trap (ATB) pedals, and (3) produces sufficient traction when having to push my bike in snow or mud. Most rain boots satisfy one or two of these requirements, but not all three. Therefore, I'll simply list the options and you can choose from them, while keeping your eyes open for better products and techniques. (I was told by two manufacturers at a recent international bike show that they were working on this problem.)

Protection during pavement riding is far easier than with ATBs, as one's off-bike (pushing) traction usually isn't critical. I've been fairly satisfied with Totes, the thick rubber shoe coverings found in department stores, as their sole holds up well to pedal abuse. However, these are heavy, somewhat bulky, and hot. This last problem brings on condensation, which, over a few hours, produces an uncomfortable, clammy feeling. Totes have therefore become my preference only for commuting.

Several bike industry companies have attempted an answer with thin shells of various fabrics. These solve the problem of weight, but most leak along the seams despite my attempts to seal them. Those that are impervious to water are fine for winter, but once again lack sufficient off-bike traction and are hot.

My answer for cold-weather touring is therefore a pair of well-sealed (with Sno-Seal or similar leather treatment) leather boots, preferably the lightweight models with side panels of breathable Gore-tex (a material with thousands of microscopic holes, too small to let rain droplets come in but large enough to let water vapor molecules pass out) or other material, covered by a breathable gaiter.

In warm-weather touring, keeping one's feet perfectly dry is not so critical. Nevertheless, I prefer this even when it is not a physiological necessity for survival. I therefore don the thin rain boot shells (unfortunately still referred to as "booties"), and simply put up with the moisture that gets inside.

A final alternative is to purchase a rainsuit with feet attached. I tested a suit like this for a Seattle-based company a few years ago, and sent it back after a five-hundred-mile ride. Like so many Gore-tex products, the suit breathed rather well, except in a driving rain (when droplets covered the holes, thereby not allowing moisture from inside to escape) and when it became soiled. Newer, improved Gore-tex fabrics are supposed to be better at this, and thus justify the steep price. But I wouldn't buy it myself, I told the company, not only for the reason of cost but because I felt like Sesame Street's "Big Bird" in the suit. A huge yellow thing, with black feet, I lacked only a beak to make the image perfect. I must admit that reaction in truck stops was enjoyable when I waddled in. But as with so many items that must be worn or used in only one kind of circumstance, the all-or-nothing suit just didn't meet the adapt-to-many-conditions requirement of clothing for the tour. Besides, it took up an entire pannier when packed away!

Gaiters (1 pair). Designed to shed water away from the tops of one's boots, gaiters attach beneath the instep (with a strap) and to the laces (with a hook), and are usually zippered up the back or side. They come in various lengths, colors, and fabrics; I prefer them rather long, red, and breathable.

Rain chaps (1 pair). These come next, as we're moving our way from the bottom up in rainwear. Cyclists have two major choices in their attempts to stay dry—the poncho/chaps combination, or a rainsuit. I use a rainsuit in midwinter riding, a poncho and chaps for all other tours. This is because of the rainsuit's problem of heat. No matter what the material is, pedal hard inside a suit and after a while you'll feel as if you're working out in a greenhouse. This makes them great when it's raining and the temperature is near the freezing point, but horrible when it's warm.

Bicycle ponchos, on the other hand, are designed to allow air to circulate around the body while still shedding rain. This works because of their unique design—pullover, tentlike, waterproof, with the back flap tying about the waist and the front with thumb loops to stretch this portion out to the handlebars. However, a hard or more horizontal rain (those days that remain in memory, when it comes in sheets blown by ferocious winds) can still soak one's lower torso, and this is where chaps come in.

Rain pants could be worn, but these close off the crotch and waist to any airflow, causing dampness inside. Chaps, however, are simple waterproof tubes that tie at the waist (to a beltloop—another reason beltless racing shorts are a pain), thereby allowing air to circulate. The chap bottoms overlap the gaiters, which in turn overlap the open portions of the shoes or boots. It is a system similar to roof tiles, with successive, rain-shedding stages or layers.

Poncho (1). Discussed above. In addition, I suggest choosing one in yellow, for the reason I mentioned earlier—this appears to be the color best seen by automobile drivers in the rain. Some ponchos also have a reflective band sewn on the backside for this purpose. Be careful to affix the hood tightly around the face, so that when you turn to look for traffic you aren't merely staring at the inside of your hood.

In addition, realize that wind gusts will be felt more severely when wearing a poncho, given the greater resistance created by such a "tent" of fabric. You'll get used to it quickly, however, and I think will find the slight loss of speed preferable to the dampness brought on by the more efficient, trimmer rainsuits.

The urethane coating makes ponchos waterproof, but some leakage can occur at the seams. "Seam Seal" and similar products should be applied at these points, sealing the threads with a transparent caulking. (Hard use can break down this seal over time; I reseal all the seams of my poncho and tent each year). After several years you might find the urethane coating of you poncho giving out. Specialty sports stores carry small cans of liquid urethane (such as "K-Kote"), which can be brushed over worn spots.

Rainsuit (1). As discussed above, I pack one only for midwinter tours, because of the heat (and thus perspiration) produced even by "breathable" fabrics. Compare the costs of these suits with that of a ponch/chaps setup, and remember that you will still require gaiters with the rain pants, unless you purchase a suit with feet attached.

Goggles (1). You only have to ride in one downpour or snowstorm to know why eye protection is necessary. Normally my sunglasses are sufficient because the lenses lighten on dark days, I try never to ride at night while on tour, and these glasses fit close to my forehead. However, a clear, very lightweight pair of plastic goggles is a good idea as backup protection. Be sure to pack them in some kind of cloth wrapping, as plastic lenses scratch easily.

Goggles (Kroops brand).

This item, like the "perfect" riding cap discussed above, can be very difficult to find. And thus I have decided in these instances to provide the names (and addresses in Appendix) of manufacturers I've been fortunate to discover. Their wares have worked extremely well for me. You may prefer others, but at least you will have one source of a good product. My preference is the Kroop's Goggles, for its extreme light weight, leather binding, vent holes (to prevent fogging), very good sealing action against the elements, and low cost. They come in many colors, but I prefer clear ones for inclement days.

Gloves (2 pairs). On winter tours I pack along a pair of very thin, lightweight gloves for warmer days (almost any fabric will suffice, though capilene liners make an excellent cool-weather outer- and cold-weather under-glove), and the warmest ski gloves I can find. You'll appreciate long and tight-fitting wrists on the warmer pair, to prevent cold air from leaking inside.

Overmitts (1 pair). It was pure delight for me when, finally, a company came out with waterproof shells large enough to fit around my huge ski gloves. I *know* you're thinking this is overkill. Well, have you ever heard of wind-chill? It refers to the effects of wind in cold weather. When air temperature and wind velocity are combined (as they are, of course, on hands and face), they produce a much lower equivalent temperature. For example, on a day when the temperature is ten degrees Fahrenheit, and the wind is twenty miles per hour, the equivalent wind-chill temperature is *minus* thirty-two degrees. And if you are riding in wet conditions (sans overmitts, in other words), the equivalent temperature is minus *seventy-four* degrees.

Face mask (1). The wind-chill discussion above should make the need for a face (or ski) mask obvious. I prefer those made of neoprene, which cover only nose, mouth, cheeks, and chin, and are secured in place behind the head with velcro. The pullover cotton or wool models tend to freeze to my mustache and beard, and are a pain (literally) to remove.

Stocking cap (1). I pack a 100 percent wool, tightly woven cap for cold days, and even find myself sleeping in it when nights are bitter. Choose one that will reach over your ears.

Jacket. For my round-the-world ride I chose down (the soft, fine feathers of ducks and geese) as the insulation for my sleeping bag and coat. What a costly mistake! I dropped feathers across two dozen countries, and with it the protection I sorely needed during the winter-Rockies crossing at the end. Fail to keep down dry, or launder it without great and time-consuming care, and feathers will ball up. Toward the end of that long ride I could hold my coat and bag to the sun, look through them, and know which spots of my body would freeze.

My next choice in jackets had man-made insulation, which, although a wee bit heavier, a tiny bit less warm, and not quite so compressible as down, nevertheless did not lose 90 percent of its insulation capability when it got wet. In fact, the man-made insulation I use now—Quallofil—*retains* ninety percent even when soaked. It worked great, but had the disadvantages of a single, somewhat bulky garment: It was still fairly large when packed, and sometimes too hot when worn, leaving me too cool when I took it off.

But the solution evolved after several more winter rides. I now pack a thinner nylon jacket whose lining is a shell (nylon outer to repel wind) of capilene or similar insulation, and, in addition, a very warm vest of Quallofil or thick capilene or polypro. On most cold days my long underwear, sweatshirt, and thin jacket are sufficient; for the coldest days in the saddle, and those immobile hours around the winter campfire, I bring out the vest for warmth. (The vest is sometimes worn without the jacket, when I'm hiking from my bicycle base camp, for instance, and wish more freedom in the arms.) The thin jacket is perfect as the only outer garment necessary for warmth for early fall and late spring tours.

Choose a high-collar jacket and you won't need to pack a scarf. The collar protects the neck up to the face mask, the stocking cap covers the forehead almost to where the mask begins.

Vest (1). Discussed above. I prefer it lined (to stop the wind when worn by itself), and equipped with a high neck and large pockets for the hands. Remember when shopping around that this is the ultimate item used in preserving core body temperature. So be sure it is *warm.*

Near the beginning of this chapter I wrote, "What follows is the clothing I pack on long rides. . . ." I can imagine female readers thinking, "That's just fine for other males, but what about us?" Well, I haven't suggested different clothing for women riders for a very good reason: It isn't different. I've toured cross-country several times in mixed groups, and taken countless shorter trips with women cyclists from their early teens into their sixties. And their clothing choices—aside from the occasional "sports bra" worn beneath sheer fabrics—simply have not been noticeably different from mine. Female commuters have told me they sometimes prefer camisoles to T-shirts beneath a blouse, but on tour this seems to be an impractical and undesirable alternative.

SHELTER AND BEDDING

Shelter

Tent (1). Begin searching for the perfect tent and you'll soon find we live in a complex world. So many choices! One-man tents, two-man tents, tents to fit a group; three-season and four-season models; freestanding or pegged; bivy sacks for simple shelter . . . the list goes on. I'll attempt to make it understandable, but you should once again prepare yourself for a lengthy search.

Of course, you could just stay in motels. Or ride without shelter, as I've done several times, and always regretted it. Rain, mosquitoes, and cold are the three banes of tentless travel. Plus lack of privacy, I suppose. And add the fears that many people have of creatures crawling over them at night.

Nevertheless, although I always pack a tent these days I don't always use it. If skies are clear and insects calm I often sleep in the open; there's something special in closing one's eyes to a canopy of stars, and awakening to sunlight. Quite often in the desert I do this, risking, I suppose, the chance that some dumb reptile will sidle up to me for warmth. But that's a relatively minor worry, given, first, the fact that no matter what so many people feel—that snakes are malevolent, sneaky things with an inborn taste for humans—serpents aren't out to get you, and, second, I think I'd sleep through the visit. (Though I was awakened once by a daring kangaroo rat, who—I swear—hopped across my chest, then stopped nearby to stare at me.)

The Moss Solet tent.

And then there's the argument for touring shelterless, which hinges upon forced creativity. I must admit that finding a place to sleep on tour, whether packing a tent or not, is one of the most agreeable times of the day. Not having a predetermined bed or place in which to spend the night is truly a vacation from the usual world. I've slept in ice houses, barns, basements, churches, attics, castles, in fields, between buildings and hay bales, under picnic tables, and behind billboards, to name a few. Most of those abodes came when I had a tent. But remove your nylon house from the equation and it means, at least during inclement weather, that you must stay *inside*.

More on this when we discuss the different "kinds" of tours. For now let's assume you've decided to carry some sort of shelter, in addition to a sleeping bag. Naturally, you want a tent that is light, stable when erected, easy to put up and disassemble, of sufficient size, waterproof, and durable. As with bikes, unfortunately, such qualities come at a cost. Begin your search with an in-person, close-up look at some brand-name tents: Moss (not the only good tent around, but a company unbeaten when it comes to innovative designs and overall quality, and the one I've used exclusively for years, except for short-term tests of other brands), North Face, Sierra Designs—compare the seams, stitching, fabrics, webbing, zippers, design, and poles with less expensive models. Give some thought to how much use you'll give it (it helps to think in terms of nights per year), and consider if long-term value makes the extra cost worthwhile.

Weight is a critical factor for cyclists, especially when one is contemplating a solo tour. (The load can be shared when there are more riders.) I'm speaking in the most general of terms, but for winter touring I try to keep my tent weight around four and a half pounds; for all other times, not much more than three. This would be relatively easy to accomplish if I weren't so completely sold on "self-supported" (freestanding) tents—those requiring no stakes to stand upright. The necessary cross-structure of poles on these tents increases their weight considerably. But the following description of a night spent wet in Utah—sent to Moss Tents along with my critique—explains why I accept the extra ounces.

> Experience—that great but ruthless teacher—proved to me one cold November that one must choose his tent most carefully when cycling in the West. We were sixty miles from any town, camped on slickrock (rock-hard sandstone) at the lip of a thousand-foot gorge. Far below lay the gray, roiling waters of the Colorado River, to which we would descend at dawn. Two days of tremendous labor had been necessary to put us at that point, but the prospect of lugging all our gear down to the water's edge—through a notch cut in the rock by pioneers a century before—promised to be harder still. We needed rest.
>
> Over the years I've used a dozen tents, and had trouble only once

in keeping one erected. The problem then was loose sand in the Middle East, when pegs pulled free during the night. But this time, in the high desert in near winter, with storm clouds coming overhead and north winds turning sharp and cold, it was impossible to make them stand for even a moment. The slickrock was hard and smooth and unaccepting; we next tied off our lines to shadscale brush, our panniers, even the top tubes of our bikes. But none of these would hold in the winds that howled that evening.

The rain began two hours after dark, great sheets of it that pummeled us in successive broadsides. We lay there cold and shivering, our tents wrapped around us like huge envelopes. Wet in an instant, we were soaked in the first half hour of an all-night rain.

You might be thinking from this that freestanding tents are great west of the Rockies, but quite unnecessary where soil covers the ground. However, self-supporters are much faster to erect (a consideration when it's about to rain), and, of course, can be used *inside* other shelter. This is done in such cases as barns and unheated garages, when warming the relatively small airspace of a tent makes sense.

While we're on warmth, consider the seasons of your travel. I normally suggest that a person buy what's called a three-season tent (with large screened areas for airflow), and just tough it out in winter. Four-season tents are heavier, and I don't like packing the extra weight. Besides, a good pad and sleeping bag will get you through.

For summer desert travel I prefer the almost completely screened tents. These are of course much lighter, but still heavy when compared to bivys. The word comes from "bivouac"—"a temporary encampment in the open, with only tents or improvised shelter"—and refers to the close-fitting sacks that serve as bug-proof, water-*resistant* sleeping-bag liners. I stress "resistant," rather than water*proof,* because, whatever the fabric, I have yet to sleep completely dry in a bivy when it rains. A savings of weight, a great loss of comfort. Once more it is a question of balance that only you can decide, but not until you have a good idea of the kind of touring you have ahead.

Bivys have a problem of condensation due to their single "wall"—one piece of fabric between the occupant and the outside. Some of the more expensive models are made of Gore-tex, improving the bivy's breathability and thereby reducing moisture inside. Tents avoid much of this problem through a rain fly, a second "wall" that is waterproof, but suspended above the pourous inner tent wall. Water vapor escapes through the first, then evaporates or condenses on the underside of the fly. With some experimentation you'll learn how much airflow is necessary inside the tent to prevent almost all condensation.

Tent size is an important consideration, especially if your tour is longer than a weekend. You'll find that all "two-man" tents are not the same size, so pay attention to the measurements given. As you did when choosing a bike, obtain catalogues and specification sheets for some deliberate, unrushed comparisons at home. Let me just add that for warm touring I pack a one-man tent; cool- and cold-weather rides bring out my two-man model—even when I'm riding solo. Why? Because of the extra gear I pack in cold weather, and because of the extra hours I'll be spending in the thing. The sun goes down very early in December, and rises late. And all those hours (once the cold has driven me from my campfire) I'm inside, reading by candlelight. At such times a little room, and a lot of comfort, are appreciated.

A few suggestions: As discussed above (under "poncho"), needle holes in fabric allow moisture to follow the threads inside. Be sure, therefore, to seal your seams. Some tourers carry a "ground sheet" to protect their tent floor from rocks and twigs; I choose to spend an extra minute combing the site for these objects, and leave the extra weight at home. Forget about tarpalins. Some riders (especially those who have never weathered a storm or insect infestation in them) suggest these simple sheets of protection as an answer to the high cost of tents. Well, you get what you pay for. Rain and bugs flock in both ends, and putting up a tarp so that it won't flap about in the breeze is a real trick.

Six inches of ripstop repair tape is good to have along, to prevent any fabric rips from becoming larger. Finally, put your tent up at home a few times before you hit the road. Your first night's idyllic camp shouldn't be ruined by the realization that you're missing half the poles.

Bedding

Sleeping bag (1). Skimp on most items for touring and you can, with a bit greater effort, overcome the problems that result. Heavier bikes require more muscle output, poor derailleurs take more time to shift. And during the day, even if you've packed insufficient clothing, you can get relatively warm by riding. But when the sun goes down and you crawl inside a crummy bag, all you can do is shiver.

The "proper" bag for a ride is therefore crucial. I carry a very lightweight, semirectangular model for summer touring ("comfort-rated" at forty-five degrees), and a modified mummy minus-five-degree heavyweight on winter rides. Now let's go over those terms.

Many riders at first think only in terms of temperature when it comes to bags. It's not a bad place to start, but don't stop there. Other considerations are shape, (rectangular, semirectangular, modified mummy, mummy), kind of fill (or insulation—down, man-made), loft (the comfort- and warmth-producing thickness of insulation), construction (sideblock baffles, differential cuts, single layers, double layer offsets, zipper draft flaps . . .), and overall weight. Let us go into each of these primary considerations, but only so far as is necessary to choose wisely. After all, you're looking to buy one, not build it.

Shape: Remember the old cloth bag you used as a kid—the one with pictures of ducks on the inside? Chances are it was rectangular, cut with perfect corners just like a mattress. These are comfortable, as they allow one to roll about at will inside. But the problem comes in heat loss. Think for a moment of what actually keeps you warm in a sleeping bag. Your body burns the fuel fed it throughout the day (in another chapter we'll get into the best kinds of foods to "stoke the furnace" at night), maintaining its normal operating temperature. You give off some of this heat; the purpose of a sleeping bag (or bed cover when at home) is simply to trap it, while keeping out the cold and at the same time allowing water vapor emitted by the body to escape. If this last point wasn't a problem we could simply enclose a thick bag in a plastic sheathing and stay warm. Unfortunately, we'd wake up soaked.

Humans have more than two million sweat glands distributed throughout the body as a means of venting off—through evaporative cooling—the excess heat created through metabolism and organ function, or acquired from the environment. Sitting in the shade on a very hot day, we lose through perspiration alone approximately a cup—eight ounces—of water per *hour*. (If we are working hard in the sun we lose approximately a *quart* per hour! Do you see why rain suits in summer don't work?) As the ambient temperature drops we lose less water, but that amount—if trapped—nevertheless will bring on wetness and a resultant chill.

That was a long-winded way to say not to wrap yourself in plastic to retain body heat. A bag's shape is one of the critical elements in keeping the warmed air around you and the cold air out. The problem with rectangular bags is, first, that it's impossible to pull the top of the bag around your neck and shoulders sufficiently to retain warmth, and, second, that your body must work harder to warm the large airspaces created by the extra room.

You will recall that I pack a semirectangular bag in summer. This shape is tapered toward the foot (reducing airspace), yet still squared off at the top. On warm nights I can therefore adjust the amount of airflow for comfort; if there's a cold snap I can bundle up in clothing and still sleep pretty warm.

(Before I forget, be sure not to trust the "comfort ratings" too completely. Your idea and mine of comfort at such-and-such a temperature might not coincide. My winter bag, for example, is, as I mentioned, rated at minus five. I have slept in it many times when it's been that cold and I *haven't* been comfortable. It does, however, preserve life in such a chill. And for that I can't complain.)

A modified mummy is tapered at the foot and closer about the shoulders than the semirectangular bag. In addition, the top is rounded to allow a close fit about the head—the spot from which we lose an amazing amount of body heat, because of blood flow to the brain, face, and scalp. Full mummies, the warmest of shapes, are body-contoured throughout. But I find them far less comfortable for sleeping than are the modified mummies, because rolling over in the things is difficult.

Fill: Earlier I spoke of the advantages and drawbacks of down, in the discussion on jackets. Once again, I would carry a down bag if I could be sure I'd keep it dry, if it were not so difficult to launder, and, finally, if the cost were more moderate. No man-made insulation is quite so compressible, quite so warm, or quite so good at maintaining loft (height of the insulating material in the bag).

But given these severe limitations (all of which I learned, at great expense, on my around-the-world ride), and the great advances over the last decade in man-made fills, I never pack down bags for touring. Remaining choices are Polarguard, Hollowfil II, Polysoft fiberfill, Quallofil. . . . I can't guarantee I'd know the difference if I slept in them blindfolded, but for my winter bag I've chosen Quallofil. It is supposed to be 95 percent as compressible as down, excellent at maintaining loft (due to the anatomy of its "tubes"; rather than simply being hollow to trap the air, each tiny tube is divided into four chambers by internal walls), and, as mentioned before, it retains 90 percent of its insulation capability even when wet (some companies claim 95 percent).

Remember that most man-made fills can be machine-laundered and dried, without fears of "clumping" as with down.

Loft: This refers to the height of the insulating material in the bag. The greater the loft, the greater the dead air space between you and the cold, thus providing increased warmth. Down has amazingly good loft; I find Quallofil very good as well. You can help this by storing your bag according to directions, which means *not* leaving your bag crammed inside its stuff sack while at home. Several commercial products are available that guarantee improved loft if used when laundering a bag (such as REI Loft II). I must admit to having never used them.

It should be obvious that a thicker bag is more comfortable, as well as warmer. Keep this in mind when assessing the importance of loft.

Construction: There's nothing mysterious about "offset quilting" and "shingled layers" when it comes to how a bag is made, but I can't see any sense in explaining each technique, especially since I'm not considering down. (With down's propensity for "cold spots," construction is more critical.) When I'm shopping for name-brand bags I pay more attention to loft and comfort rating, and assume the construction is all right. But if I'm considering an inexpensive bag produced by a company with little history, I look for *why* the cost is less. With some bags the reason is obvious—the fill is simply dumped between two large sheets of fabric, instead of being sewn into individual compartments. Buy one without these compartments and you'll find your insulation uneven, especially after washing.

However, no matter who the manufacturer is, I *always* look for what's called a "zipper draft flap" or "insulated draft tube"—a protective piece of insulation to prevent heat loss at the zipper junction. I also make sure the zipper has large tabs (or handles, to be found easily at night), does not bind or get caught easily in surrounding fabric when closed, and is of good quality (YKK is one very good and popular zipper brand). For those of you who will be traveling with a partner, be sure to buy bags with right or left zipper openings, so that two bags can be zipped together for a warmer sleep. Finally, the draw cord (at the shoulders on a semirectangular, around the head on modified and mummy) should be placed conveniently, operate smoothly, and come equipped with an easily released lock.

Overall Weight: Don't get confused by "fill weights" when looking at the specifications of sleeping bags. That term refers to just what it says—the weight of the insulation only. It is an important consideration, especially when comparing bags. But what you'll feel while pedaling is found in the "total weight" column.

My summer bag is light—barely over two pounds. My winter sack tips in at about four pounds, eight ounces. That is heavy, making my shelter and bedding load almost ten pounds by itself. But when it's December, at night, in the cold, I don't begrudge an ounce.

Ground pad (1). A good pad is a necessary part of your attempt to have a good, restful sleep. In cold weather it insulates your bag from the freezing, wet ground. And at any time of year it is far more comfortable than hard earth.

I find the most comfortable pads are the relatively heavy air mattresses. Unlike the solid, nearly indestructible closed-cell ensolite foam pads, however, these can be damaged. In fact, I managed one evening to acquire *four* holes in one. And all I did was pull it close around the campfire, and fail to notice the smell of burning plastic as the airborne embers melted my bed. Brother.

Naturally, I don't blame the pad for my idiocy. But I found that not all the specially made patches held over the holes, and that my inner tube vulcanizing kit patches were worthless in the attempt. Now, I wish to make it clear that I know hikers and tourers who have carried these mattresses for years without a problem. Due to the length and often remote regions of my rides, however, I choose not to chance it.

At about one-half the weight, and a quarter the cost, closed-cell foam pads are the popular alternative to air mattresses. Excellent at insulating the sleeper from the ground (though not quite so good as air mattresses), the closed-cell pads are far less comfortable. I've never found it difficult to sleep due to discomfort from the ground, but you might borrow someone's pad and try it out before you buy.

Open-cell pads also exist, and are much softer (and therefore more comfortable) than closed cell kinds. However, they also insulate less well, weigh a bit more, and damage far more easily. (At this writing I am about to test the "Ridge Rest" closed-cell pad, called thus for the ridges of foam that are supposed to give the comfort of open cell, and yet provide "valleys" of air between the ridges, which are said to trap the body's heat. I can't say yet if it works, but the theory sounds good. Take a look at them before you buy.)

Beyond construction, you must decide upon pad length. "Regular" length is about five feet, leaving either your head or feet hanging over the end. "Long" pads are about six feet in length, and thus insulate a person more fully from the ground. It seems an obvious choice, at least in cold weather. But that extra foot of pad costs one between a third and half a pound. I normally pack the shorter pad and simply insulte my head or feet with clothing.

PERSONAL ITEMS

For Beauty's Sake

Towel (1). A small, thin hand towel is light and dries quickly. And you're wrong if you think it's insufficient for the job. Just change your technique. After washing, wring out your washcloth and use it as you would a towel all over your body, wringing it out each time it becomes saturated. You'll be amazed at how dry you can get with this alone. Complete the task with the towel.

Washcloth (1). Thin, to dry quickly.

Soap (1 bar or bottle). Soap can be a real pain on a ride. The most convenient by far are the biodegradable "liquid suds" varieties that come in a leakproof plastic bottle and double in purpose as shampoo (a rather rough one, I might add). On a short ride these are fine, but resupply on long rides is difficult, and I'm always having to resort to the usual soap-dish/soap alternative after a week or more. You could start off with a larger bottle, but the extra weight is tough to justify.

My preference is the hard, biodegradable (*always*) bar soap found in outdoor equipment stores. I use this also for washing out my clothes.

Soap dish (1). I prefer the soft plastic or aluminum type with a top that slides over the container base. Most plastic dishes have three small plastic "hinges" that break after a time, thus requiring a rubber band to hold the thing together. Bad design. Pack it in a heavy-duty ziplock plastic bag, and you won't have suds inside your pannier.

Toothbrush (1).

Toothbrush case (1). You'll find "travel toothbrushes" that come packed inside a tiny rectangular case. I don't care for these, in that the toothbrush shank is too short and I have to shove half the case into my mouth to reach back teeth properly.

Toothpaste (1 tube). I was delighted when the first soft plastic tubes were invented, for the old metal tubes were not only heavy but cracked over time, leaving paste inside my handlebar bag. For years, therefore, I carried tooth powder, but have replaced this with the far more convenient plastic tubes.

Comb (1).

Toilet paper (partial roll). I pack about twenty sheets or so, folded and kept dry inside a ziplock bag. Resupply is easy, at cafés. An extra nickel on the tip will cover costs and salve your conscience.

Deodorant (1). We all have a preferred brand that works best with our particular body chemistry, and a kind (roll-on, stick . . .) that we like more than others. My only suggestion is to avoid the heavy glass containers of some roll-ons, and the aerosol cans of sprays. It gets mighty hot inside saddle bags.

Shampoo (1). It is reported that some mountain men and Indians cleaned their hands of grease following a meal by running the fingers through their hair. I have my doubts, but if true it must at least have kept locks supple. Too bad that our tastes in hair styles have changed.

"Beauty" now requires a modicum of cleanliness, necessitating yet more weight on tour. I pack a very small "sample" bottle of shampoo and use it sparingly. Try out the combination soap/shampoo alternative before relying on it while on your ride.

Waterless hand cleaner (1). Great for ridding yourself of grease after repairs. I pack one 35mm film cannister of it.

Nailbrush (1). I'm always amazed at how people jump on me about this particular "luxury." Not only when I give "bike touring clinics" and discuss my equipment list, but even in numerous letters from readers, I am taken to task for arguing for lighter loads while recommending packing a nailbrush. My defense is that the things weigh only grams, and the luxury of cleanliness at such a little cost is well worth pedaling a wee bit harder.

Fingernail clipper (1). This or a metal nail file should go along for the ride, especially on week-long trips and even on shorter rides. For a while I used only the metal file of my Swiss army knife, and saved the weight of yet another item. But I felt like a barbarian. And after keeping a careful tally over the years as to how often I used my heavy Swiss army, I finally jettisoned the thing, at least for domestic rides.

Medical Supplies

Sunshade (1). I learned the hard way that even a well-tanned body can still burn. It happened to me in the Middle East, after months of pedaling to get there. I've also been surprised in our own desert Southwest, and when cycling high in the mountains. Now I ride wearing at least a T-shirt, and pack a small container of medium-strength sunblock and/or suntan lotion, depending upon the region and my own skin condition. If you are planning a summer ride, begin exposing yourself to the sun in spring. And be sure to tan that area a couple of inches below your belt in back; this spot is normally hidden from the sun, but becomes exposed when in riding position.

Aspirin (20). Packed in cotton in a 35mm film cannister, to avoid finding only white dust when you reach for a headache cure.

Snakebite kit (1). Suction cups, scalpel, disinfectant, tourniquet, and directions that should be read *before* you have a close encounter of the serpentine kind.

Desitin (1). An antiseptic cream which I find better than all the rest in relieving the pain of sunburn and abrasion. Again, one 35mm container full.

Band-Aids (10). Curled up inside a 35mm container.

Butterfly closure bandages (6). Of various sizes, packed with the Band-Aids. These are shaped as one would expect from the name, and serve as temporary stitches in times of severe cuts.

Gauze compress pads (6). The cyclist's problem with most commercially prepared first-aid kits is the insufficient amount of gauze padding therein. You will probably never experience it, but bikers' wounds are usually large-area surface scrapes, resulting from a fall. I therefore pack a half-dozen or so 4″×4″ pads; they come individually packed in sterile paper packages, and I then enclose the lot in a ziplock bag.

Gauze (1 roll). Used to keep the pads in place, and as a bandage if the wound is too large for a Band-Aid, and too small for a pad. Pack in ziplock bag.

Ace bandage (2). Great for a weak joint. These can also be used to hold compress pads in place when the gauze roll is needed elsewhere.

Benadryl (1 package). Formerly a prescription drug, now sold over the counter. I carry this antihistamine to guard against an allergic reaction to something I might meet (or eat) along the trail.

Insect repellent (1 bottle). A plastic bottle, of course.

Water-purification tablets (1 bottle). Most thin-tire tourers will never have to treat their water. Nevertheless, I take tablets just in case. They won't get rid of Giardia, but are helpful against many other malevolent creatures. (For long, backcountry mountain bike trips, however, I pack a filter-system water purifier; these screen out Giardia, and thorough boiling kills it. The unwelcome Giardia protozoa should be feared in *all* untreated water. It is a nasty intestinal disease, and takes a long time to leave the body.)

Moleskin/second skin (1 pad). I carry a 2″ × 2″ pad wound inside a 35mm cannister, for application to tender spots *before* a blister appears. "Second skin" is a similar product sold by Spenco.

Miscellaneous

Pocket knife (1). At long last, major manufacturers have developed extremely lightweight knives. Gerber, Buck, Tekna, and others now offer trim, excellent blades that weigh but a few ounces. My personal favorite is the "Bucklite" model, for its excellent edge-holding ability, extremely strong lock-blade device, and the fact that I required only a bit of practice to flip it out one-handed (switchbladelike). You never know when you'll want to impress an orange.

Sunglasses/case (1). Fail to carry a belt-mounted case and you'll probably end up buying a second pair of glasses along the trail. I finally had a saddle maker produce a crushproof leather case for me; it now joins me for every ride.

Concerning the glasses themselves, I like variable-shade lenses that do not distort natural colors. They are not so dark as many others, and somewhat more of the sun's rays come through. But in this manner I can wear my sunglasses always, and not have to switch to goggles until the rain begins. Many people do not like the feel of glasses, and avoid them even when on a bike. But let me warn you: Glasses are a good idea whenever in the saddle, and especially on tour. Catch a single junebug in the eyeball, or strain your eyes after days of sunny skies, and you'll know the importance of having a shield of glass or plastic between you and the world when traveling at good speed.

I would like to add, however, that there is little need in my opinion to cover half one's face with lenses. For some reason a current fad in cycling eyewear is plastic wraps that rival lycra tights in color and bike jerseys in lack of form. I don't want to sound as if I were beating a dead horse, but time and again I encounter riders who resemble insects in their dress, and have paid a lot to look that way. Fashion is a personal matter. However, don't be surprised when your designer touring togs exact a social cost on tour.

Flashlight/batteries (1). My preference in this category has evolved with the options, which increase every year. I've gone from "mini-mags" to "flexible heads," to the lightweight beauties of today that fit around the skull (with expandable stretch strap, and thus free the hands for putting up a tent in the dark. These "cordless head lamps" require two AA batteries (avoid the four-battery model, to save weight), and pack their own replacement bulbs.

Camera/film (1). Well, one camera for most of us, and as much film as you wish to carry. When I am on long rides I pack "mailers," enabling me to send my film off for development and thus free myself from the weight. I have found that most cyclists shoot slides, not only for the cost savings but because this allows them to share their rides with others on a wall. If slides and slide shows are your preference and you expect long, hot days in the saddle, allow me to suggest that you pack Kodachrome. Unlike Ektachrome, which is sensitive to heat buildup in panniers, Kodachrome is basically a hardy black-and-white film until the color-coupler stage of lab development.

Rope (15'). I prefer parachute cord (usually available from army surplus stores) for its tensile strength and light weight. If you can't find it I suggest a *thin* nylon braid. Rope comes in handy as a clothesline, emergency shock cord, snare. . . .

Ripstop repair tape (6"). I talked about this before, under "tent." It allows you to keep a rip in the tent wall or floor from getting any larger.

Matches (one box). I prefer the large kitchen matches, their length trimmed to allow packing in a waterproof film cannister. Look closely and you'll notice a much thicker wooden stem on these matches that that found on "waterproof" or most other kinds; this provides a better and longer burn, necessary sometimes to start a fire.

Notebook (1). You'll need something (carried inside a ziplock bag) in which to list the names and addresses of people you meet, places you've been, things you've seen and done. I know, you think you'll remember it all distinctly. Guess again. Start out with a little spiral pad. You can always buy a larger one if necessary.

Book (1). Small, paperback, preferably Melville. (I'm joking about the author, though he's just about my favorite whether at home or on the road, *and* he does, after all, speak to travelers. Like you, Ishmael, in *Moby Dick,* is beginning an adventure. And when he writes of sleeping in an unheated room, the air ice cold except beneath the covers, he seems to be describing what I've felt so many times on winter tours inside my tent: "Then there you lie like the one warm spark in the heart of an arctic crystal." What an image.)

Pen (1). A new one, with lots of ink. And though you've probably not considered it before, they do come in greatly differing weights.

Safety pins (10). Different sizes, packed in cotton, inside a film cannister. They will allow a quick repair of clothing, until sewing time in camp.

Sewing kit (1). I now carry a single, rather large curved needle, and a spool of army surplus "No. 0" suture. It's tougher than any thread I've found.

Cup (1). I almost never pack a stove,* and thus my cup is a heavy steel, nearly indestructible, Sierra Club model that serves as soup pot/coffee cup/oatmeal bowl. This works far better over an open campfire if I also pack the extremely convenient and lightweight (aluminum) "backpacker's grill," but I do this only in winter and then only if it's a real backcountry tour.

*Stove. I've asterisked this item because of what I said above about "almost" never packing stoves. Many tourers do, however, and because I have carried them in the past and will again on future backcountry rides, I will provide a few personal notes of guidance.

The "big three" factors when one considers a stove are type of fuel, weight, and cost. In the first of these categories the choice comes down to butane, white gas (Coleman or similar brands), and multifuel stoves (they burn white gas, kerosene, and sometimes alcohol). As you should expect by this point of the book there are pros and cons in all corners.

Butane is by far the most convenient, for the fuel comes in cannisters that are simply plugged into the stove and fired up—no priming or pumping required.

Disadvantages are the extreme high cost compared to white gas (roughly nine dollars per pound versus seventy cents), slightly poorer availability of cannisters, the need to keep the cannisters warm in winter (I put one in my sleeping bag at night), and the fact that they must be packed out even when empty (empty cannisters weigh about 2½ ounces, full ones 8½ ounces). Of course, you can always choose to leave them scattered along the road, an alternative that many people unfortunately prefer.

White-gas stoves have to be pumped. I find this an extremely minor chore requiring, usually, only a few seconds. Preheating is necessary with some, but

Stoves (left to right: Coleman Peak 1, MSR Whisperlite, Roberts).

this involves merely the burning of a flammable paste along an inlet tube or the firing of a small pan of gas. I have found that these workhorses boil water faster than butane does. Fuel is plentiful and cheap throughtout the United States and Canada, but less available overseas.

Multifuel stoves are the most recent entries into the market, and make for a wise choice if you anticipate traveling abroad. But I suggest you use white gas when it is available. Kerosene is oily (spills will not evaporate quickly) and has an unpleasant smell; alcohol burns only half as hot as white gas and butane.

Most of my personal experience has come with the Hank Roberts (butane), an MSR WhisperLite and Coleman Peak 1 (white gas), and the Coleman Peak 1 Multi-Fuel (white gas and kerosene). I can recommend all these as excellent stoves—they have given me long and true service. However, in my opinion the early model Coleman is just too heavy for cycling; the Multi-Fuel model is a full third lighter.

Concerning the third category of cost, I will leave that up to you and your Yellow Pages, except to say that you will probably find the Roberts by far the least expensive.

I carry both my WhisperLite and the Colemans inside the two-part aluminum Coleman "Cook Kit." The larger "pot" serves in the morning for oats, in the evening for soup; the smaller holds coffee always. When there's no café nearby and none in sight for days it is heaven to roll out of the sleeping bag and fire up warm food. You'll have to pay for the pleasure in increased weight (19 ounces, empty, for both the MSR WhisperLite—with external fuel bottle— and Coleman Peak 1 Multi-Fuel: Hank Roberts weighs 8 ounces without cannister), but sometimes it's worth it.

All stoves provide the warning in their operating instructions. Even so, I'll add it here: Do *not* operate any model stove inside a closed tent or too close to the wall or roof. Not only might you have to re-shingle when the flame flares unpredictably, but you might not live to do so. Carbon monoxide is a by-product with every stove; good ventilation is a must.

Utensil set (1). Lexan plastic. It's inexpensive, light, and lasts forever.

Can opener (1). I'm still carrying the same little GI opener I got on my first day in 'Nam in 1968. That should be sufficient testimonial. Civilians can get them at sporting-goods stores.

Pants clips (two). I prefer metal bands to velcro straps, for their greater convenience. (Well, to be honest, also for their history. Metal clips were used by cyclists around the turn of the century. Yes, they're a bit heavier than straps, and aren't as reflective, but the link with the past more than compensates.)

Map (1). More on this in Chapter 7.

Compass (1). Critical on mountain bike trails and dirt roads, I also carry one on pavement tours for occasional help in orientation. Some time ago I received a letter from a reader who asked how I managed to avoid destroying my compass when knocking it about on rough ATB rides. The answer is to buy quality (like the fluid-filled Brunton model I prefer), place it in your handlebar bag or pannier in such a manner that it doesn't bounce about, and avoid dropping it.

Candle lantern (1). I've tried many different kinds of illumination techniques over the years, for the hours of reading in winter tents. And I have never found anything better than the simple metal/glass globe candle lantern. The dripless candles burn brightly for eight or nine hours, and the lantern

Candle lantern.

itself weighs only five ounces in aluminum. I bought the slightly heavier brass one, however, for its beauty.

If it is a short trip, or summer (with such long days), or if you're with fellow riders and thus might not be reading very much, you'll probably choose to save the weight by taking only the flashlight suggested above.

Two years ago I tested a liquid fuel candle lantern, and I found it to be more trouble than I needed. This was, however, a purely personal rejection, by which I mean that the product did work. I was sorry at my decision, for a separate metal ring can fit on the top, turning the unit into a tiny stove for heating one's coffee. Lukewarm, in about an hour.

Candles (2). Sometimes I lug along as many as eight, if I won't reach a large town or my postal resupply point for a month. Be sure when you buy that these are the long-burn, dripless kind, and of the proper length for your particular lantern. (By the way, I don't waste my kitchen matches on the simple lighting of a candle. Every now and then I pick up a book of cardboard matches from a café, and pack it for convenience in the protective lantern pouch.

Watch (1). I usually do not carry a watch when on tour, unless the ride is one involving a great deal of ferry-catching or other such "timed" events in towns, or on one-day (no camping gear) rides when knowing how many hours of daylight remain is important to getting home. But I am often asked, at the end of slide shows and bike clinics, to name a watch that will withstand the weather and abuse. In the old days my watches performed poorly, as they fogged, drowned in an all-day rain, or, with the early battery models, simply got too cold and quit ticking.

But things today are different. For a fraction of what I once paid I can now obtain an analog watch that not only takes the beating in stride, but provides sufficient luminosity to tell the time in a dark tent, adds a moveable bezel and alarm, gives the day and date, and even has a chronometer for timing workouts. I've been drowning the same Casio sports model (supposedly good to a hundred meters deep) now for longer than I can recall, and it has worked like a champ. Again, I am not saying that other models won't do as well. But at least this way you know the functions I have found useful, and a brand from which to begin your search.

We're through. And you're probably thinking it won't fit into a car trunk, much less a few panniers. But have faith. You will learn in the next chapter where to pack it on the bike.

4

Loading
the Touring Bike

Tent, sleeping bag, clothes, food . . . where in the world does it all go? I can't blame you if you're thinking it won't fit, or that the weight of this gear will make the bike feel as if you are pedaling a mule. But, as I said earlier, don't despair. In this chapter we'll get it all loaded, and later you will be supplied with tips on how to accustom yourself to pedaling a road-ready bike. So cheer up. Besides, we're discussing the civilized sport of cycle touring, not the beastly notion of strapping that weight to your back.

LOADING THE BIKE

Load distribution is a relatively simple matter, perhaps best approached with a few easy-to-remember rules:

1. Weight should be relatively even on either side.

2. Weight should be distributed between the front and rear of the bike, in roughly a one-third/two-thirds proportion.

3. Whenever possible, weight should be carried low and close to the frame.

The reasons are, I think, obvious.

Loaded touring bike: 1) handlebar bag, 2) front pannier, 3) water bottles, 4) fenders, 5) seat bag, 6) tent, 7) ground pad, 8) sleeping bag, 9) rear pannier, 10) toe clip/strap, 11) spokes (taped to chainstay), 12) mirror, 13) pump (normally mounted on frame)

1. Pack more weight on one side of the bike and you'll spend all day leaning in the opposite direction. More important, you're damaging your spokes.

2. Put too much weight over the rear tire and you'll damage your rim, snap spokes, and feel when pedaling that you're dragging your luggage behind you. Put too much weight in front and steering will feel sluggish and difficult.

3. Bike handling is greatly improved when weight is low and close to the frame, as the center of gravity is lowered and the bike when turned or leaned acts as a single unit, riding in tight profile over the tires. Centrifugal force keeps a bike and rider upright when in a lean; hang a lot of weight on the outside of panniers and you're giving gravity a better chance to end your ride. Weight carried high on a bike also causes difficulty in braking, as the load is above the brakes and tends to shift over them and to the front.

Those are the rules. Now let us discuss the real world of breaking them.

I spent much of 1984 (and several months of each year since) testing various thin- and fat-tire pannier systems, including the excellent Robert Beckman Designs (formerly Needle Works) bags. Bob Beckman, the owner and designer of that line, had discussed with me the reasoning behind his system's lack of a handlebar bag. With considerable conviction he argued that this is the worst place for weight on a bike, as it conflicts with both braking and the steering axis.

So I tried it, during a five-hundred-mile retracing of Sherman's March from Chattanooga, Tennessee, over the rough hills of northern Georgia to Atlanta, and on through the tidewater plain to Savannah on the coast. What a ride! And Bob was right; the bike did handle beautifully. There is not, in my opinion, a more perfectly engineered bag/rack system than Beckman panniers on Bruce Gordon racks. As I mentioned in Chapter 2, the racks ride like chromoly extensions of the frame. And the bags—designed specifically for these racks—couldn't be more stable if they were glued into place. (Robert Beckman Designs bags are now available for the standard Blackburn-type racks as well as Gordons.)

However, I missed my handlebar bag. To me the convenience of this location (for my camera, snacks, tape recorder for road notes . . .) more than offset the decrease in steering ease. The answer was simple; on my next ride I added another company's bar bag, and worked at keeping the load in it small. Once again, decide for *yourself* which system is preferable.

Now, time for specifics. Item placement changes for me somewhat with each set of panniers I test, but in general my bike is loaded as follows:

Handlebar Bag

    camera
    a few rolls of film
    toothbrush/paste
    notebook (if very small)
    pen
    map
    compass
    watch cap/riding cap

Seat Bag (under the saddle)

    poncho
    chaps
    saddle cover

rain boots (this is a tight fit, even with the larger seat bags now available; but nothing beats this location for quick access when a shower erupts; if your bag can handle only one of these items I'd choose the poncho first, next the chaps, then the rain boots, as I find I don this gear in these three stages as rain severity increases; as I'm less concerned for the dryness of my saddle than how wet *I'm* getting, my saddle cover is in the seat bag if there's room, in a left rear pannier pocket if not)

Rear Panniers

tools

clothing; whichever system you devise for yourself to organize your clothing, just make sure to even out the load, and to place lighter items toward the outside of the bags)

medical/miscellaneous (in those saddlebags with outside pockets I place the items from these lists that need to be most accessible: first-aid gear, rain covers, toilet paper, flashlight, etc.

bike parts (low in the bags, held close to frame just as tools)

On Top of Rear Rack

tent (usually the heaviest item of one's entire load, I pack it perpendicular to the rack length, and closest behind the saddle; it is best to have this weight forward of or at least directly over the rear axle)

sleeping bag (packed directly on top of rack, behind tent)

ground pad (the lightest and smallest of these three items, it is packed highest—on top of the tent and bag)

Front Panniers

food (I prefer to keep my right front bag devoted almost solely to food, utensils, cup; this allows me, first, to know immediately where all such items can be found; second, to lay my bike down—*always* on the non-derailleur side—without fear of smashing the fruit or loaf of bread; third, to keep from fouling other gear with food)

personal (front left pannier; small items packed inside single nylon bag, to make it easy to carry all at once to the creek bank or shower room of a campground)

On Top of Front Rack

> folded clincher tire (attached to top of rack with extra shock cord)
> jacket/vest (in waterproof stuff sack, resting on top of the folded tire)

This is a general guide only, of course, to the placement of gear which your own riding style and pannier system will demand. Personalize your packing, but keep in mind the earlier "rules" of proportionate weight front and rear, equal weight side-to-side, and heavy items low and close-in. (Several panniers come equipped with "compression straps" to cinch the load closer to the rack.)

After a week of touring, or several short weekend rides, you'll come up with a load system that works well; at this point make a list of where each item is packed. It will help you greatly in packing for next year's first ride. Also, make a list of "problems" after each tour, so that you can fix them before the next trip. I know you think you'll remember them until the following spring; if you're like me you'll remember most, but not all. Bikes are elegant, simple, quiet creatures, able to speed you silently through the countryside even while carrying all your gear. It's a shame when a single zipper tab or metal D-ring, clanging against its fellow or the rack, spoils the day's perfection.

A few more notes on packing:

1. Be sure that all stuff sacks and rain covers are fully waterproof. Seal the seams in the same way you did the tent floor and fly. Also, nylon sacks used inside the panniers to keep certain items together (shower items from the "personal" list, for example) need not be waterproof or heavy. Remember that you'll be pushing the total weight of your bike and gear across the country, not just the bag contents.

2. Place all easily damaged fruit inside a disposable plastic bag (I keep my old breadbags for this purpose). Toss an unbagged pear inside a pannier and you'll find only hours later that road shock has smeared it over everything else in your pack.

3. For dirty clothes take along *two* lightweight nylon sacks—one for each rear pannier. If you have only one such sack all unwashed clothes must be carried in one bag only, thus requiring that clean clothing or other items be transferred to the opposite-side pannier to maintain proper weight distribution. And once you begin changing the location of items—even if "only for the day," you'll never know where to look for things in a hurry.

4. Whether you carry a stove, or (as I prefer) use a single metal cup as your

cooking gear over an open fire, you'll want to protect other items in the same pannier from soot. Again, a nylon or plastic bag will come in handy.

5.   I mentioned in an earlier chapter the extremely important factor of handlebar bag suspension. Shop around. You'll find you can carry far more weight in a well-designed bar bag, and with less shimmy, than in a lightly loaded poor one.

6.   One of the best things about traveling with a partner is the overall weight savings. One rider packs the tent, another the tools, and so on. Just be sure that both riders have a snakebite kit and a minimum of first-aid gear, and that the rider more often pulling up the rear packs the tools.

7.   Peanut butter and jelly should not of course be packed in their glass jars. Outdoor sport shops often have wide-mouth, screw-lid, unbreakable plastic jars that serve as perfect containers. I use rather large ones, to pack a good supply for weeks backcountry; determine the quantity you'll need before you buy.

8.   Begin a ride with extra ziplock plastic bags, as you'll find them perfect for cheese, soap dish. . . .

5

Riding
the Touring Bike

OVER THE YEARS I've been with many people when, for their first time, they pedaled a loaded bike. And from almost every person I've heard the same exclamation: "Yikes! It's so different!"

It is. But then, so is a car equipped with manual transmission, compared to an automatic, and you got used to that. The key was that someone (if you were lucky) told you what to expect, and then let you practice. It's the same with a bike. I'll provide several paragraphs of warnings; it is up to you to give yourself a few weeks of practice. In case you're thinking of skipping this break-in period, read the following true story of a rider who felt a loaded bike just couldn't be *that* different.

> We had traveled by bus to the starting point, and on that first morning straddled our bikes and prepared to mount up. But then came trouble. One rider, trying to pedal out of the parking lot, could not control her bike. Here we were, a thousand miles from home and three times that from our destination, at the end of a six-month period of preparation for two months of touring through some of the most difficult terrain in North America, and one member of the group had not ridden a single mile with her bike fully loaded for travel. Sick at heart for this inauspicious beginning, we dismounted and watched as the rider circled the lot for forty minutes, trying to accustom herself to the weight. But, if I

was sick at watching this and all it portended for the next few weeks, it was nothing compared to my emotions when she finally wheeled back to us, unsteadily dismounted and said, "Well, I can stay on the bike now. I just can't shift gears."

Decreased maneuverability, increased stopping distance, muscle strain, saddle discomfort—all are complaints of the cyclist who in a single day moves from weight-free riding to full touring load. The obvious solution—to work up to this weight of twenty or thirty pounds incrementally and over time—is believed and obeyed by surprisingly few riders. I'm not saying the intent is absent; in most cases the decision is made (usually on that first warm day in spring), but not carried through to action. It is like planning for one's retirement—the savings plan starts tomorrow. But while "tomorrow" never arrives, the tour take-off date does.

In the next chapter I will move you through a training program in which I suggest riding with partial load, then half, then full touring load for more than a month before a trip. By beginning with only a few pounds you can gradually accustom your body to the strain, and your reflexes to the necessary changes in riding technique.

Some cyclists think they can get the same benefit of load-training by simply pedaling a bit harder. But a loaded bike causes one to push back harder in the saddle, demands more upper torso power on hills, catches winds that blow from every angle (but especially from either side, pummeling saddlebags as if they were the side of a barn), requires changes in anticipated braking distance and, if one is riding with a handlebar bag, obscures a rider's view of his front wheel.

These differences seem minute if encountered over time, enormous if faced all at once. The choice is yours.

RIDING SAFETY

Thus far I've discussed only the muscle strain one will feel if beginning a tour without the benefit of practice at riding a loaded bike. But it doesn't take much imagination to foresee other possible problems. It is true that cycling has been termed "soft" (nondamaging) exercise, to differentiate it from the accumulative physical abuse often acquired in sports like jogging. (As you will find when pedaling into a head wind or up a steep hill for the first time, "soft" does not mean "easy.") There are some ways, however, that you can hurt yourself on a bike. Most common is the one that comes immediately to mind when "bike safety" is heard—collisions with automobiles.

But there are also the falls one can take by leaning incorrectly on turns, using brakes improperly, or hitting sewer gratings or other urban road obstructions. As you already know if you ride a lot, avoiding such pitfalls soon becomes second nature; I'll discuss them briefly for beginners, and also to remind us old-timers not to become so cocky that we forget the caution required to keep us upright. But there's another way to court injury when cycling, one that is of special concern to tourers. It is the tendency to push high (hard-to-pedal) gears early on in riding with a load.

Wise cyclists avoid this problem by "spinning," a technique referring to the pedal cadence of so many revolutions per minute (that's *pedal* revolutions—two per full turn of the crank). Racers as a rule spin much faster than tourers. Their common range is from ninety to one hundred plus; tourers are most often in the seventy to (sometimes) high eighties range. There are a lot of "expert" opinions on the "best" spin rates. But few disagree on one point: Drop much below seventy when packing a load and you're both pedaling inefficiently and asking for knee damage.

I should admit that I am at the low end of "acceptable spins," a rate that many racing and recreational cyclists consider woefully inefficient. But injury is one thing, efficiency another. I avoid the first by analyzing my last twenty years of touring; I don't pursue the second if it gets in the way of my *travel*. Granted, a higher spin rate can become almost second nature if practiced long enough. But, for me, it never becomes so natural that I'm not thinking about it at least a bit. I therefore concentrate on pedaling completely "around the circle" (a phrase in biking that refers to using the feet and ankles and toeclips/straps to pull up on the back pedal while pushing forward and down on the front), and keeping my spin rate high enough (by dropping into a lower gear than the maximum I can handle) so as not to feel that I'm pushing too hard with the legs.

Another boost in efficiency comes when using the foot as a powerful fulcrum during pedal rotation, through a technique known as "ankling." It is tiring at first (proof that muscles in the feet and ankles are being brought into play), and a bit awkward, and tends to be used less when one's spin is high (I find myself ankling more when tackling tough hills or pedaling into head winds). But it can become very natural with just a little practice.

Begin by adjusting your saddle height so that when the pedal is at the end of its down-stroke (six o'clock), it is too low for your instep or heel to reach it easily. Just the ball of the foot should be in place. (However, do not raise the saddle so much that when pedaling your hips rock back and forth a great deal.) At the top of the up-stroke (twelve o'clock) the heel should be *below* the pedal; the foot is actually pointing up slightly at this time. Now, on the beginning down-stroke (actually a forward motion at first, then down; remember that you are pedaling "around the circle" and not just up and down), not only the thigh and calf muscles, but those in the foot and ankle as well, will be used for propulsion.

To give you an idea of how natural such pedaling can become, after riding for many years with clips and straps I raced off to a class one day with bare pedals. I'd been working on my bike, hadn't watched the clock, and didn't have time to slap on the clips without being late. What a surprise! My rear foot kept coming off the pedal on the upstroke, so much so that I was forced to concentrate on keeping it in place. Until that time I had no idea how much power I added through "lifting" the rear pedal.

Work on higher cadence and ankling and you'll avoid the "heavy legs" feeling so often associated, needlessly, with cycling. Two other techniques will also help. Don't forget to gear down before coming to a stop. Even when I'm riding a stripped bike I drop into my second largest freewheel sprocket at these times; the low gear allows me to zoom off across the intersection as soon as the light turns green, thereby not taxing my legs or the patience of drivers behind me. The second technique is one I employ only when riding mountain bikes, but many fellow tourers find it helpful. This is to stand in the pedals when going up a steep hill or starting off from a dead stop at the bottom of one. Your body's weight will then assist leg muscles in pushing the pedals.

At the risk of boring you I will now mention a few safety tips which, though commonplace to most of us, deserve a few minutes' thought. First, get into the habit of raising the inside pedal when leaning into a curve. Granted, tourers do not lean as radically as racers, but one's pedal can still strike pavement if it's in the six-o'clock position and you're riding below the "crown" or high point of the road.

Watch out for doors when passing parked cars in towns, as the hard-to-see occupant might open it quickly. Attune your ears for the dull metallic sound of doors, and your eyes for the head of the driver (difficult to see behind headrests) and the tell-tale dip of the left shoulder as the driver reaches for the handle. The decreased maneuverability of a loaded bike makes evasive action slower, besides pushing you farther into the street. When possible I ride a door's length from parked cars, but not if this places me in traffic. You will read articles now and then in bike magazines stating that we have a "right" to the road, and therefore should "claim a lane" no matter how many honking motorists are behind. I agree with the first part, that we do belong there. But civility, common sense, and the instinct for self-preservation argue against a single rider's blocking the flow of traffic.

In the early sixties many communities across the country still had rules about bikes traveling against the flow of traffic. This is no longer the case, but ask about it when licensing your bike (licensing is a good idea for identification purposes in case of theft, and another justification for our "right" to a piece of the road); or call the nearest police station. And when on tour play the averages by riding with the flow, and over to the side or on the shoulder. This is where road debris collects, and where sewer gratings (storm drains) wait for unsuspecting narrow tires. But what's the choice? I'd rather have a flat than disappear beneath a Buick.

Inclement weather, dusk, and dawn are rough times for tourers. Wait until sunup to begin pedaling, pull off the road before dusk. And when in rain or snow be sure *not* to trust a motorist to see you. Wear your goggles to keep your own eyes in good shape, ride slowly and defensively, and don't lean as much into turns. Slick streets and wet leaves can cause thin tires to slide out from under you.

Most tourers' traffic problems, of course, come about in urban areas. But even rural riding has its share. Narrow, shoulderless two-lane roads are rough on us *and* motorists; don't forget that it's no fun to drop from fifty-five miles an hour to ten behind a biker when waiting for a chance to pass. Recognize that from behind the wheel a driver sees only that you aren't on the shoulder, which his tax money built at great expense, while from where you sit the horribly rough surface is in plain view. Unless there is glass or a hole that might toss me from the saddle I make it a practice to drop onto the shoulder when one motorist is behind me and a second car is coming at us from the other lane. If the shoulder is smooth I'm already there. And make sure to use it (or the far right inches of the road if shoulderless) just beyond the tops of hills when you hear traffic coming from behind. Drivers at such times cannot see you until they're only seconds away, and you are risking a lot on their reaction time if you fail to stay to the right.

Many highways have a pavement drop-off half an inch or an inch deep between the regular road surface and the shoulder. It is easy to negotiate this when riding solo (by striking this "lip" at an angle), but first-time group tourers can have troubles when drifting over it while riding double. Conversation is the primary joy of companion travel, but keep your eyes on the road. Know ahead of time who will drop behind when cars appear, and get into the habit of having the outside rider place himself so that his front wheel parallels your rear. In this position you can hear each other easily, and the outside rider can fall behind in a flash when necessary.

I mentioned earlier the greatly increased braking time of loaded bikes. Keep the brakes aligned close to the rims (thereby reducing by split seconds the application of rubber to wheels), use both at the same time and with equal pressure, and practice pulling your rig to a fast stop before you have to do it on tour. There is one time, however, when I do not use both brakes simultaneously. This is when I'm in snow or on ice. I find that the application of my rear brake under these conditions causes my rear wheel to slide, a movement I find very difficult to control. The front wheel can also slide when its brake is used, but I can control this far more easily through the handlebars.

Another problem in group riding actually occurs when all pedaling has stopped. There is a tendency for groups to cluster on the shoulder of the road, often with rear wheels or more still in the flow of traffic. You may be taking up only a few inches, but you are increasing—for no reason—each passing motorist's concern.

No discussion of bike safety is complete without at least a mention of helmets. I could provide statistics about cycle touring's being far safer than playing football or skiing or flying to a vacation spot. But we all recognize the existence of chance in the world; no matter how carefully we ride there is always the possibility of being struck by a car or making contact with the road. And this is where keeping your skull intact becomes all-important.

When you are on a bike there is simply no other part of your body as crucial to your overall health *and* as vulnerable to injury as your head. The arguments are sound in favor of wearing helmets, no matter what their heat and weight. Besides, tremendous strides have been made in recent years to increase airflow, decrease weight, improve protection, and even make the things more stylish. Remember, too, that the ugliest of helmets still looks great when compared to a coffin.

I have made these arguments many times when suggesting the use of helmets, and put them before you in all sincerity. I do not, however, wear one myself. And, unlike many people, I do not see an incongruity. I've had folks wag fingers in my face about the bad example I set by riding bareheaded. My response is always the same: all reasons against wearing a helmet are silly except one—the individual's right to decide for himself whether he wishes to take that risk.

Without getting into a long debate let me just anticipate your comeback on helmets for motorcyclists and seat belts in cars. When I owned a motorcycle I wore a helmet, and I always belt myself in cars. Why the difference? Because I see a far greater risk in those instances, because I'm in cars and on motorcycles far less than on bikes and I do not wish to strap on a helmet fifteen times a day.

Again, my suggestion is that you consider carefully the use of a helmet. Add a rearview mirror and reflectors to your bike, stay to the right, and don't ride too fast, and try now and again to see the world from the motorist's point of view. Do these things and we all have a much better chance to enjoy life and remain with the living.

Right: Linda Prosperie enjoys a Backroads Bicycle Touring ride in Canada—
and proves that one can look good in a helmet.

6

Diet and Exercise

For all the time spent pursuing and consuming food, the average American knows *very* little about what goes into his mouth—and even less about what happens after that. Any cyclist concerned with general health and good performance cannot afford such ignorance. Once past the tongue, food becomes no more than fuel. To carry a metaphor appropriate to this chapter, *you* are the bike's engine, taking in calories that are then transformed into the energy necessary to propel you down the road. It is not simply a matter of how many calories are required; amount is important, but the *kind* of fuel matters also. A well-tuned, high-octane ride is impossible when you're only burning regular fuel.

Let me dispel one fear right off the bat: Your appetite will *not* increase dramatically if you begin a cycling program. In fact, active people tend to eat in proportion to the calories burned. And, though it's hard to believe, regular exercise actually decreases one's appetite overall.

Why do I bring this up? Because no matter how good cycling is for the body, not many of us would do it if it made us fat. All that fantasy of how biking is hard work, how it brings on big muscles that will turn to fat when we're older, how we'll eat like a horse and stretch out our stomachs and never be able to eat less—even if we stop exercising—is bunk.

I'll tell you something else. The "no pain, no gain" philosophy of exercise is also untrue, and has done a lot to discourage partial converts to exercise from trying it. Who wants to hurt? On a bike that fits you, and which you're riding correctly, you'll feel good during and after a workout.

One more bit of information to carry you through the following words on nutrition: Any diet plan that doesn't include a *permanent* altering of eating and exercise habits just won't do the trick. You might starve yourself and look good for the summer, but come fall the weight will be right back in place.

Cycling can be your key to permanent weight control. There is the aerobic (endurance) benefit from this form of exercise that is so easy on the body's joints. There is the wonderful mental and physical feeling of well-being flowing from such exercise. And there is the calorie-burning-yet-enjoyable time in the saddle, which keeps you coming back for more. Little willpower is necessary when you like the process.

Let's begin with some basics. "Calorie"—a word in everyone's vocabu-lary—is actually a unit measurement of heat. Specifically, it is the amount of heat required to raise the temperature of one kilogram of water one degree Centigrade. But (thank Heaven) for our purposes here it refers to the energy production of a food. In other words, if you eat a high-calorie cookie, how far will it propel you down the road? And, for many of us who also like to ride, train, and tour because of the slimming effect it has on the body, the term "calorie" refers to the "weight potential" of a food. In this respect our question is how hard we'll have to work to "burn" it off.

All of which makes energy production and weight loss pretty simple, right? Just count the cals coming in and be sure they're sufficient for your output (to have the energy necessary for your training or tour route), or insuf-ficient if weight loss is the goal.

If it was that easy, supermarket shelves wouldn't offer dozens of "nutri-tion" and "weight-loss plan" books. The "kind" of food—not just the number of calories—is important for anyone who wishes to stabilize or lose weight, while at the same time maintaining or increasing energy output. This makes basic food knowledge critical to touring cyclists.

I began my cross-country cycling as a sophomore in high school, and thus merely applied what I'd learned about nutrition in health class to eating prop-erly on the road. On that first ride, back in 1965, I kept in mind the "four basic food groups" and tried to eat from all of them: (1) meat/poultry/fish/eggs; (2) milk/other dairy products; (3) bread/pasta/grains; (4) fruits/vegetables.

It all worked pretty well. I was eating a relatively balanced diet, acquiring the vitamins and minerals necessary to provide internal organs with the chemi-cals necessary for function. And my youth, and the increased food quantities overall, compensated for my ignorance concerning how I could have helped my body with a more specific diet.

Today, decades later, I'm still pretty lackadaisical when it comes to food. Olympic cyclists might search out health food stores in the towns they pedal through, or weigh each helping of granola, or pass by apple pie in favor of bean sprouts. Not me. But I have learned that just a little care about my body's fuel while on tour and in training can produce excellent results. It is with this experience of my personal improvement in performance—not a trendy obsession with diet, or a mantralike belief that "you are what you eat"—that I offer the following advice.

It is generally accepted that a diet of roughly 65 percent carbohydrates, 20 percent fats, and 15 percent protein provides an excellent balance for cyclists. Carbohydrates are needed for the quick energy they provide. In contrast, protein isn't broken down as fuel for muscles, but is necessary in the structure of muscle tissue. Although fat is broken down for energy, it takes far longer for the body to do this.

Thus the great importance of carbohydrates to energy-seeking cyclists. There are actually two kinds of "carbs"—simple, and complex. Simple carbs are those found in fruit and sugar, which go quickly to the muscles as glucose (blood sugar). Complex carbs are found in whole grains, pasta, vegetables, and legumes (peas, beans . . .). These are critical in that they break down more slowly than simple carbs, thus providing the body with what is called a "more constant burn." This means that, unlike the quick energy/quick letdown one gets from simple carbs, complex carbohydrates are the source of a continuous supply of pedal-turning energy. Obviously, combining the two will get the rider off to a good start, and carry him to the end.

But the body makes the task somewhat difficult. For, although it can store enormous quantities of fat, it can store (approximately) only a two-hour supply of carbohydrates. Therein lies the need to provide it with easily digestible complex carbs while riding. You'll get the "constant burn," plus the important fiber, vitamins, and minerals in these foods. And by eating this level of carbs—65 percent or so of total intake—you will be cutting down on the fats that are so much more difficult to shed. Not only do they require far more time to digest, but every gram of fat equals some nine calories; each gram of protein or carbohydrate equals only half that.

With a few more facts we can see why good nutrition, combined with regular cycling, is an excellent plan for weight control. Biking is a tremendous aerobic exercise, if you ride as outlined later in this chapter. Not only will you be burning simple and complex carbohydrates during your ride, and conditioning muscles, lungs, and heart, but the body also turns partially to the energy-production mode called beta oxidation—the use of stored fats.

It makes sense that we would burn more calories during exercise. But for once our bodies seem to be working with us on weight control. For this increase in calorie consumption does not stop when you quit pedaling. Studies indicate that the body continues to use up calories more quickly for *many* hours after exercise. Happy days.

Here's another term. "Basal metabolic rate"—your BMR—tells you how fast you use stored energy while resting. You need to know it so as to find how many calories you use each day just in living. A simple formula for this, for determining how many calories you need just to maintain your current weight, is fifteen calories for each pound of weight for a man, twelve for a woman. Purchase a table of caloric food counts, compute your daily total caloric intake, and compare it with your necessary "maintenance calories." If you eat at a "maintenance loss" of five hundred calories each day you'll lose approximately a pound a week (roughly 3500 calories to a pound of body weight).

In fact, with an hour of cycling daily you can maintain your food intake at current levels and still lose that pound. Riding at a cruising speed of about twelve miles per hour burns up more than eight calories per minute, or approximately five hundred every hour. If you alter your diet from high-fat to high-carbs you'll lose even more.

However, if weight loss is one of the primary reasons you have begun cycling, know what to expect. After a few weeks of training for a tour you will probably notice the beginnings of a new look, as muscles become toned and excess fat is trimmed. The *look* is there, but the bathroom scale reads as before. What's up?

The answer is that your new, lean muscles weigh about five times as much as fat. You're right; it isn't fair. But remember that you can choose to tone and shape as you wish, depending upon how much you change your overall food intake, the kinds of food you eat, and the amount of training you do.

In the next section I shall discuss specific foods for training and the tour, water loss and replacement, heart rates and glycogen stores. If you are serious about permanent weight control you will benefit greatly from what I once derisively termed "calorie-conscious" cycling. If you're interested only in the training, weight control will come naturally. It is an enjoyable path to a good tour *and* excellent physical health.

The evidence is all around us. A British physician's report speaks of the health potential of exercise when it is moderate, continued throughout life, and sufficiently vigorous to bring on slight breathlessness. We see proof of that daily, in the vibrant look of active people of all ages. We feel the truth of it ourselves, in the zip in our step when we're in shape, the colds we manage not to catch, the better mental attitude that comes as an unexpected by-product of being fit.

Now a *New England Journal of Medicine* report goes one step farther: Moderate exercise actually adds years to a person's life. Sceptics once believed that because healthy people chose to exercise, they of course lived longer. But a study over two decades proves otherwise; one is healthy *because* one exercises. Even more impressive, death rates of active individuals range from one-quarter to one-half less than that of the least active.

In short, moderate activity—like cycling—both prolongs life *and* improves its quality.

So how does one get started on this road to health? Well, you're taking the first steps now, by spending time learning how to fit a bike and ride correctly, eat the best foods, and be safe while in the saddle. After that comes the exercise itself—how much, how little, how often. Let's begin with that now.

Most experts in this field suggest that if you have been inactive for a long time, and especially if you are in your thirties or older, are a bit overweight, smoke, or have high blood pressure, you should have a checkup by a physician before beginning an exercise routine. Once that is behind you, take out a pencil and figure out three "heart rates" of extreme importance.

> The first is your *maximum heart rate,* a figure determined by subtracting your age from 220.
>
> The second is *training rate,* which refers to the level at which you must bring your heart in order for aerobic fitness to begin. For this you must first take your pulse upon awakening in the morning, to find your "resting pulse." Then subtract this number from your maximum rate, multiply the result by .6, and add the resting pulse to it again.
>
> The third is *maximum safe rate while exercising,* which comes from subtracting your resting pulse from your maximum rate again, multiplying by .8 this time, and adding your resting pulse to it.

It sounds confusing, but what you wind up with is a couple of critical numbers—the second and third ones—that will act as training guides for you.

For instance, let us say you're thirty-five, and have a resting pulse of 60. Your maximum heart rate would be 185; your training rate 135; your maximum safe rate while exercising, 160.

(A second common method of finding training and maximum pulse rates, one that is much simpler but I think slightly less accurate, is to subtract your age from 220, then figure 65 and 80 percent of that number. You should try to keep your pulse between these two numbers while exercising.)

You can now begin working toward the important "aerobic fitness" (endurance) level by bringing your heartbeat between 135 and 160, for a minimum of thirty minutes three or four times a week. When you start out in your exercise program, shoot for the heart rate closer to 135. After a few weeks, when you're feeling more fit, push toward the 160 figure. You'll notice quite a drop in your resting pulse rate as you reach aerobic fitness. (An easy method of feeling your pulse while working out is to lay two fingers on the neck, next to your Adam's apple.)

Good. You've computed the training range you'll be shooting for, and have a bike that fits you well for the task. We shall hit the road in a moment, but, first, a few more words of theory.

As speed is not particularly crucial to cycle touring, aerobic fitness is much more important than anaerobic (power) fitness. The latter is a necessary goal for racers, acquired through the "sprint" training technique of periodic all-out bouts of frantic pedaling. Yet, although required far less often, tourers have an occasional need for such power, as when pulling tough hills with a load. We can slow down if we have to, but getting off to walk is a time-consuming pain, and sometimes rough on the ego. Power training is therefore worth discussion, and—depending upon the terrain of your next tour—worthy of at least part of your in-saddle training time as well.

While climbing steep or very long hills with a touring load you will notice times that you're nearly out of breath. You've reached what is called your "anaerobic threshold"—the point at which insufficient oxygen is reaching the muscles. Muscle cells begin using fuel in a different manner at this point, and a waste product called lactic acid is created. When too much of this collects, you'll experience cramps.

With proper training, however, this "threshold" can be pushed back considerably. Bringing yourself to the "training rate" through constant, enduring action at an exercise level below your maximum potential, builds you up aerobically. But anaerobic training requires hill storming or other hard-work periods for a minute or so, to increase the flow of blood and oxygen to muscles.

This can of course be accomplished while on your bike taking hills. But recently I acquired an exercycle, a Schwinn Air-Dyne, which makes both forms of training extremely convenient indoors. You'll hear more about this machine in the mountain bike chapter, as its unique position among exercycles—in offering an upper- as well as lower-torso workout—makes it perfect for acquiring the greatly increased arm and shoulder power necessary for ATB touring over rough terrain. At present, however, we're interested primarily (though not at all exclusively, as you'll find out from sore muscles throughout the body if you don't begin training slowly) in lower-torso endurance and power. The advantage of the Air-Dyne, or of any other well-made exercycle equipped with at least a timer, odometer, and rpm (revolutions per minute) speedometer, is, first, that one can train whatever the weather, and, second, that the gauges make it extremely difficult to lie to oneself.

Whether on the road or aboard an exercycle, it is best to begin slowly and

Willa Huelskamp, tourer and bike shop manager, keeping both upper and lower torsos in shape on a Schwinn Air-Dyne exercycle.

continue at this pace for at least a few minutes before proceeding to heavy exertion. This increases the internal temperature of one's muscles, and thins the fluids inside them, expanding the muscles' stretch capability by as much as 20 percent. (Flexibility, the third necessary goal of a cyclist's training program, is discussed below.) The risk of injury is thus greatly reduced.

Once warmed, I bring my pulse to the training rate and maintain that level for five minutes or so. If I am on the Air-Dyne I then pretend I'm on the road fully loaded, facing a 12 percent hill. I pedal hard for a minute (or all-out for thirty seconds), then return to my training-rate level. After a while I can index my pulse rather accurately by the control panel rpm speedometer (or ergometer—"work load" indicator), and thus won't be sitting there with fingers on my wrist or neck. By the way, there is another benefit from indoor exercycles: They allow one to read or watch the news during a workout, thereby removing one more reason for skipping a training session.

On the Air-Dyne I pedal for twenty minutes, then put my feet up on the "stops" and work the arms alone for a final ten minutes. The total aerobic workout is thus a half-hour. I enjoy jogging, and thus alternate my exercycle

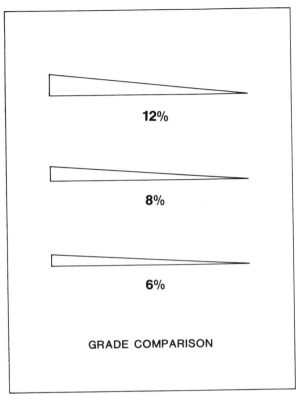

12%

8%

6%

GRADE COMPARISON

Grade comparison. A 6% hill indicates a six-foot rise in elevation for every one hundred feet of linear progress.

days with days of forty-five-minute jogs. But I give up the running for at least the last two weeks before a trip, substituting hard, fully loaded road riding when possible, exercycle workouts when it's not. This period allows my body to become accustomed to the load and the changes in handling brought on by weight, and it lets my posterior get to know the saddle once again under the increased strain of weight.

Let me add something here about motivation. Throughout this chapter I've suggested *permanent* alterations in diet and exercise as the ultimate goal. The short-range task of getting in shape for a tour is in comparison easy for most people; the motivation is apparent, and looms ever larger as the take-off date comes near. But how to maintain that sleek, new look, the result of a couple of weeks on the road? For me, physical fitness is a requirement of work; if I get out of shape I can't cycle six months each year, which means I don't have the photos and stories that make up my living. Which would mean I'd have to get a real job. Yet, sometimes I have to push myself to work out. Why?

It is a fundamental philosophic problem, one that I pondered long before seeing the light. The answer is, of course, that Man has a natural tendency toward sloth. A proper corollary is perhaps that Man's natural tendency toward sloth increases with age. Some might argue a connection between the growing listlessness and the skepticism that appears to come with middle age, but that's idiocy. The only connection is that skepticism is a fashionable excuse, to add to the list of others, for our natural state of ennui.

At least that's true for me. And the way I have fought it is to realize the validity of the old maxim, "Man is a creature of habit," and used it in my favor. Simply, I forced myself to work out until it became habitual, and now I allow my propensity for habit to fight my propensity for sloth. (My lifelong habit of watching the national news also helps out, as I can use my exercycle during that same half-hour.)

Sloth would still have won out, however, had I not discovered another basic tendency of Man. We will sometimes exert ourselves to have fun. That makes things a bit easier; make sure you enjoy the exercise you choose to stay in shape. If you didn't enjoy cycling you wouldn't be reading this, and so we can assume you will be making a two-wheeled approach to better health.

More truisms: We will sometimes exert ourselves to feel good physically and mentally, to look good, to receive compliments from fellow workers and friends, and to avoid the pain that comes, ultimately, from physical inaction. We're in luck—for cycling brings on all these things. And all therefore contribute to putting and keeping us in the saddle, week after week, year after year.

Back to training for a tour. Remember, first, that there's no need to train for the *Tour de France* if your ride will consist of only thirty miles per day. Whatever distance you plan on averaging—thirty miles, fifty, seventy-five, a hundred—your training should be set up so as to have you pedaling these miles easily, fully loaded, at the beginning of your tour.

A second thing to remember is that the best kind of training for a ride is riding. Unfortunately, even with the increasing daylight hours of spring (the season most people get into shape for a tour), the obligations of work, school, family, friends, and the like often take up too many of our precious daylight training hours. Once more I'll make a plug for indoor exercycles (sometimes called stationary bicycles, though they have a single wheel), or the popular windtrainers or rollers, which make cycling an anytime sport.

Windtrainers, which are considerably less expensive, most often have a device for locking your bike's fork in place (front wheel removed), and a roller in back on which the rear tire sits. This fan-blade-equipped roller provides resistance through the force required in displacing wind, thus the name windtrainer.

"Rollers" are differentiated from exercycles and windtrainers primarily in the skill required to ride them. The bicycle's wheels sit between dual sets of rollers; there is no fork-locking device to hold the bike in place. This requirement of balance is most attractive to racers, as it teaches smooth pedaling and

Bob Welsh stays in touring shape through two-wheeled commuting;
notice fenders, handlebar bell, U-lock on front rack, Spenco gloves,
and pants clips.

attention to nuance. I, however, find it to be a drag, as I can't pedal sloppily while turning the pages of a book.

I'll get into the use of weights and rowing machines in the mountain bike chapter, but for now will suggest that the general tourer can get into "road shape" quite well without the use of such physical fitness "devices." Riding, and good all-round health, are the keys to success. With this in mind I'll offer an *extremely general* twelve-week training program, designed for the rider who wishes to be able to tour an average of thirty-five to fifty miles per day. (Just increase mileages if you'll be averaging more on tour, decrease if you'll be covering less ground than that.) I developed it long ago for those who became interested in touring on that first warm day in spring, and wished to leave on tour as soon as they (or their kids) got out of school. It has been kept extremely general to allow each rider to "personalize" it to his own beginning-ability level.

TWELVE-WEEK TRAINING PROGRAM (all exercises to be performed daily unless otherwise indicated)

Week One

Calisthenics. Think back to your high school or military exercises, the push-ups, sit-ups (with knees bent), jumping-jack routines you endured. Use five repetitions (reps) of each at first just to get the blood stirring.

Riding. Two to three miles of easy terrain, with only the weight of a "commuting bag" (poncho, a few tools) on the bike.

Walking. One-half to one mile at brisk pace, if you don't have your bike yet.

Stretching. As discussed below, quarter-hour minimum throughout training program.

Week Two

Calisthenics. More reps than in first week if possible.

Riding. Five miles easy terrain, commuting bag only.

Jogging. Short distances interspersed with walking if you don't have your bike yet (and only if you have proper footwear), or your usual jogging routine; remember that, though jogging will prepare you aerobically for a ride, it does nothing for riding skill, doesn't accustom your posterior to the saddle, doesn't exercise the upper torso muscles at all, and works on muscles differently than does riding; in short, do not allow jogging to take the place of riding in your training schedule. (I should perhaps add that many people think that jogging is better for you—aerobically—than riding. But they're wrong. The cardiovascular benefit of a half-hour ride and a half-hour jog is identical, if the heart-rate level is the same.)

Stretching.

Week Three

Calisthenics. Increased number of reps from week two, less rest time between exercises.

Riding. Five miles easy terrain, commuting bag only.

Stretching.

Week Four

Same as Week Three.

Week Five

Calisthenics. Ten reps each, no rest between exercises.

Riding. Ten miles easy terrain, commuting bag only, increase speed slightly.

Stretching.

Week Six

Calisthenics. As in Week Five.

Riding. Ten miles moderately hilly terrain, fifteen miles flat terrain if no hills around; eight to ten pounds on bicycle; pedal normal speed this week to become used to weight.

Stretching.

Week Seven

Same as Week Six (except to increase pedal speed slightly).

Week Eight

Calisthenics. As in Weeks Six/Seven, though concentration from here to end will be on riding and stretching; omit calisthenics if their inclusion would otherwise require shortening time spent riding/stretching.

Riding. Ten to fifteen miles easy terrain; half of expected touring load; begin working toward "training rate" discussed above.

Stretching.

Week Nine

Riding. Ten to fifteen miles hilly terrain (thus beginning of "power" training, but do not push high gears on the hills); half touring load; training rate when possible.

Stretching.

Week Ten

Riding. Ten miles fairly easy terrain; full touring load (primary goal of this week is to accustom oneself to additional weight on bike; do not push toward training rate).

Stretching.

Week Eleven

Riding. Twenty miles hilly terrain (aerobic and anaerobic training both will come from pushing load over hills; if no hills available, increase pulse to training rate and occasionally push harder for sixty to ninety seconds); full touring load [daily, if time permits; at least alternate days].

Stretching.

Week Twelve

Riding. Same as Week Eleven, except for "shakedown cruise" of weekend overnight ride, fifty miles both days with full touring load.

Stretching. If you have allowed yourself to get out of shape, the daily riding distances will probably seem extreme—in both the effort and the time required to accomplish them. But remember that you're working up to that level, not beginning there; and that by that time you'll be riding easily at between ten and fifteen miles per hour average, even with tour weight. Even the twenty-mile rides, therefore, will take you only about ninety minutes.

One good way to combine training and a busy schedule is to commute by bicycle to work or school. You will be saving time *and* money, by the way, for recent estimates put the per-mile-driven cost of a compact automobile at a whopping forty-four cents (and rising annually). In my usual commutes I find that medium-speed, safe city riding brings on very slight breathlessness, especially when going uphill. I'm reaching the lower range of my aerobic "training rate," am working out the body's musculature, accustoming myself to the "contact points" of hands, feet, and bottom, and am riding at about the same speed I'll be doing on the tour. I can also pack as much weight as I wish, to increase the workout, and add a few miles to the route if desired or cut back on them (if schedule demands) by driving part of the distance and pedaling the rest.

I dress in loose-fitting clothes, and cool down by pedaling slowly for the last two blocks; this notion of two-wheeled commuters requiring shower facilities at work is simply one more excuse for maintaining a slothful approach to life. Before writing full-time I taught school for several years, and in spring would simply arrive a quarter-hour earlier, use a washcloth on my upper torso and don a fresh undershirt. Clean, fully awake, and feeling fit, I was ready for the energy-sapping onslaught of America's youth. Then the ride home helped soothe the tensions sufficiently to avoid a well-deserved ulcer.

Let me add a warning, however, to those who might see commuting as a perfect time to train hard. You can't train hard on an unloaded bike without riding hard, and in all but the most hilly terrains this means *fast* riding. And there's no way in urban jungles that you can ride fast *and* safely at the same time. I've already told you that riding with weight is a whole new ball game, one that you'll lose if your spring training is spent unloaded and just pedaling fast. So load up, and slow down. Too much speed in the city will just get you creamed.

Food

Let's take a breather from the exercises to move back for a moment into our discussion of food. Try to burn the wrong fuel while training and even the correct technique will count for very little. Remember that the body has only about two hours' worth of glycogen—the stored form of glucose (the blood sugar used by muscles for fuel). Remember also to replenish this glycogen store with a high-carbohydrate diet (especially those long-lasting complex carbs—foods that contain starch and "naturally occurring sugars"). And don't wait until you're hungry to eat, for the body requires two to three hours to break these foods down into fuel. (Bananas, apples, and dried fruit will begin supplying energy within an hour of consumption.) "Eat before you're hungry, drink before you're thirsty," is a wise old cyclist maxim.

Long-distance cyclists usually find that four or five smaller meals during the day, with several high-carb snacks between, is far better than three large sleep-inducing meals. The time spent eating these meals allows the body to begin breaking down the carbohydrates, to bathe the muscles in a near-constant source of fuel.

Eat a lot of fats before you board the bike and they'll sit in your stomach, due to their very slow digestion rate. Not only is your body unable to make use of their fuel potential, but you'll feel terrible.

You'll feel far worse, however, if you starve your body of necessary glucose. The resultant condition of low blood sugar is called hypoglycemia, but is more often termed (unfortunately) "the bonk." It is, simply, the inability to continue—no power to pedal, and a hollow, listless feeling overall. The answer is, to stop, eat, rest. Pay attention to your body during training, to see which foods (and in what quantities and time periods) work best for you.

When I was a kid I was told that a candy bar before a game would improve performance on the field. I didn't pay close enough attention to see if it
worked; it seemed too good an excuse to eat something I liked. Unfortunately,
this palatable theory has been debunked. *Don't* load up on high-sugar foods in
an attempt to raise your blood-sugar level. Why? Because large amounts of
sugar cause the pancreas to release insulin, which in conjunction with riding
hard will drop the glucose level rapidly for a short time. Momentary weakness
sets in, exactly at that point when you expected a lift.

Another problem for touring cyclists is water intake. Two-thirds of the
body is water, and if this amount is not maintained, things go wrong. Oddly, we
often fail to register thirst until we're already slightly dehydrated. As with the
need to eat before we're hungry, cyclists should drink before the tongue tells
them to.

But how much? Well, a human working hard in ninety-degree temperature needs approximately ten quarts (that's two and a half gallons!) of fluids every day. If you're in an arid climate little perspiration will be noticed,
though sweat loss alone equals a quart an hour even if you're barely pedaling.
Fail to get enough water in you and you'll feel listless and sleepy.

Any liquid is good for you if you reach this dangerous point. Yet most
commercial soft drinks have far too much sugar—more than 10 percent. We
already know what too much sugar will do to the body. Some cyclists prefer
slightly sugared water, but keep it diluted to about 2 percent. Personally, I don't
bother with it. Many books and articles are filled with suggestions of "energy
bars" and "fructose dilutions," which would have you spending half your time
out of the saddle mixing up fancy elixirs. I simply try to eat from all four food
groups, pay attention to what doesn't agree with hard riding, remember to
stoke the furnace often with complex carbs (especially on cold winter nights in
frosty tents), and drink a lot. If I'm eating well I assume I'm ingesting sufficient
vitamins and minerals. But if it's the standard backcountry fare of peanut butter, jelly, bread, and cheese (my dried fruits go so quickly!) during a long
mountain bike ride far from towns for resupply, I take a multivitamin each day.

You will notice advertisements for "electrolyte replenishments," some of
which make you wonder how you lived till now without them. Yes, I munched
salt tablets in 'Nam, and ate a lot of bananas (read "potassium") when cycling
Kenya and India. But Stateside has been a different story. I may be wrong, but
I do notice a certain increase in desire for salt when I'm pedaling deserts, and a
true craving for fruits and vegetables in hot-weather touring anywhere. Again,
some riders suggest one-eighth teaspoon or so of salt in a water bottle if you
perspire heavily, added to the sugar mentioned above. I've never found it necessary, but that doesn't mean you won't. Chances are you'll be your own best
doctor if you pay attention to results.

Almost all athletes today build toward what is called the "triangle" of physical fitness: strength, endurance, flexibility. Whether a professional football player or Olympic cyclist, these three key elements are crucial to success.

Unfortunately, many beginning cyclists have the mistaken idea that they need only strength and endurance. They can see the need for strength, to storm hills while on tour, and the requirement of endurance for long hours in the saddle.

But flexibility? How flexible must one be to bike? Aren't you just sitting there in one position, with only legs moving about?

Athletes have a saying: "Strength creates motion, flexibility permits it." Thus you may have plenty of muscle power to pedal all day long, but if those muscles and connecting tissues—and the joints that muscles hold together—aren't able to stretch and flex easily, your ride will be cut short.

Knowledgeable cyclists have therefore learned the need for an off-the-bike routine of stretching exercises. These should be done very slowly and smoothly, *not* with the bouncing, jerky movement sometimes seen when people bend over to touch their toes. Why? Because nerves in the muscles cause an automatic reflex when stretched too far, too fast. This can be seen best by watching someone nod off to sleep. The head falls forward, then jerks up quickly. Neck muscles had been stretched too quickly, and reacted by contracting to pull the head back into place.

Yet when muscles and their tough surrounding sheaths (fascias) are warmed and elongated slowly, their stretching ability is increased by as much as 20 percent. (Most cyclists therefore stretch *after* a ride, choosing to limber up in the saddle by pedaling slowly for the first few minutes of a training ride or day on tour.) Attempt to relax the muscles as much as possible, then assume one of the exercise positions discussed below and stretch, slowly and smoothly, until you can feel it. Go easily, for pushing the limits of pain in stretching can tear muscle. As with strength and endurance training, it takes time to become fit.

Flexibility naturally decreases with age. I was in my mid-thirties when stretching became habitual for me, but my quarter-hour daily workouts soon had me feeling looser than I had felt for a decade. Joints can move through a fuller range of motion, the body is less injury-prone (both in use and in case of fall), and long, elastic muscles are able to produce far greater force than inelastic ones. The promise of somatic pleasure and increased performance should be sufficient to make you give stretching a try.

[I choose various routines from the following exercises, depending upon my training style and type of ride. I normally hold each position for thirty to sixty seconds, granting the full minute to tighter muscles. Each position is employed only once during a workout, unless the affected region is particularly tight. As with the question of "how to tour," there is no *single* accepted "best" way to stretch. So pay attention to what works for you.]

1. *Neck stretch:* Drop the chin toward the chest, then tilt the head straight back as far as possible. Turn upright head full right, then full left. Lean head over one shoulder, then the other, as if attempting to touch either ear to shoulder without moving shoulder up toward it. Finally, roll head slowly in complete circle, first in one direction and then in the other.

2. *Arm swing:* Not a calisthenic, this should be done very slowly, one arm at a time. Begin with arm straight out to side, raise straight above, then move forward in complete circle, stopping at each ninety degree point to hold for ten seconds or so while stretching arm out in that direction as if straining to reach something. I end by giving both arms ten moderate-speed full-circle swings.

3. *Standing thigh stretch:* Locking knees, bend over from waist to touch toes (after a month of this I was able to put full hands flat upon the floor), then grab back of ankles and pull head toward knees. Return to upright position, bend backward, then to both sides.

4. *Sitting thigh stretch:* Sit with legs fully extended, bend forward and grab ankles, pull downward.

5. *Kneeling thigh stretch:* Kneel with toes extended. Keeping thighs and upper torso in line, bend backward from the knees.

6. *Lower back stretch:* Sit with legs crossed before you. Lean over legs, touch elbows to floor.

7. *Abductor stretch:* (muscles on inside of upper thigh) Sit on floor with legs bent at knees and soles of feet together. Keeping back straight hold both feet, bend from waist, pull torso forward.

8. *Sitting side bend stretch:* Sit with both legs outstretched; pull right leg up, placing right foot on outside of left knee. Turn to the right by placing left arm on outside of right knee and pressing against it. Repeat it other direction.

There is one final technique—self-massage—which I employ on occasion after a particularly tough day on tour. My own process is more of a kneading than anything else, using the thumb and first three fingers to move deep into and loosen the muscles of my lower calf, upper thigh (front and back), and lower neck. Massage encourages blood flow to and from muscle, working thereby as an excellent restorative. Most important, though, is that the self-massage, like all the training and eating tips in this chapter, *feels* good.

Work on making the whole notion of staying fit a habit. I promise you'll enjoy the bounce to your step, the self-respect that comes from an energetic life. And remember what I said early on about exercise increasing the quantity of life.

Improved quality; increased quantity. What a deal!

7

Planning The Tour

I CAN STILL RECALL sitting at my parents' kitchen table in the spring of 1965, planning my first cross-country tour. Before me lay all the items I felt necessary for the task: pencil, paper, an insurance company atlas with one page devoted to each state—at the scale of one inch to each forty miles. Like most such "flat" maps there was no indication of elevation change. Kansas and Colorado were identical.

The choice of destination and the route-planning process were simple. My buddy and I had never been on an out-of-state vacation; we'd have pedaled our three-speeds anywhere and loved it. By chance—a geography class that year on the Great Lakes—we made Lake Superior our destination. I therefore merely ran a straight line from our home in St. Louis to the lake's western tip, ran another from the eastern side back to home, then searched my tiny atlas maps for noninterstate highways closest to that route. Next, I added up the round-trip mileage, and divided this by eighty, our estimated miles per day (mpd). (Somehow we'd gotten the notion we could average approximately ten miles an hour fully loaded, and guessed at eight hours' saddle time daily.) In this manner we were looking at roughly three weeks' road time. Figuring total expenses of three dollars per day, we each left home with sixty bucks.

It didn't take long to realize we had goofed. The short, steep hills along the Mississippi came by the hundreds and combined with head winds to slow down our laden bikes. I had assumed it would be slightly cooler since we were

Roy Longuet and me (left) in 1965, standing in front of the Keokuk, Iowa, jail (where we were spending the night); my first long tour—1700 miles in 21 days. Note three-speed bikes, backpacks, wire basket on Roy's bike, heavy chrome fender on mine, small bottle of ammonia (for dogs) on my handlebars, and the huge canteen that served as our common water bottle.

heading north, so I had packed a windbreaker; in Iowa, one-sixth of our total funds went for insulated underwear. (We had no long pants; the thick, quilted underwear was therefore worn beneath shorts and T-shirts. I still wince at the memory of stares from passersby.) And rain? Well, I won't go into it.

Youthful exuberance and dumb pride made us reject route alterations. This factor, and the hunger brought on by our fixed, tight budget, required that we maintain our miles-per-day average, whatever the terrain. It was a rough first taste of cycle touring. Nevertheless, I returned with a love for the road and two good lessons provided by the hard experience of that journey: Begin planning early, thoroughly, *creatively;* and be *flexible.*

The first task in planning is to decide on what *kind* of ride it will be. In other words, whether it's a single night on the road or a hundred, do you plan to camp? Stay in motels/hotels/hostels/jails/barns/garages/ice houses? Or do both? My own style, and thus my suggestion for you, is the third option—the "combination" tour. In this manner one has the greatest flexibility possible. A motels-only tour requires reaching one's reservation; a camping-only ride will push you out of cities and large towns every nightfall. But pack your own

Left: Daryl Schueller touring the tough hills of northern Georgia.

abode (tent or bivy, sleeping bag, and ground pad), plus the funds necessary to rent a room occasionally or the creativity to find a free roof of some kind, and one more element of a "disciplined-time" life has been escaped. Chance conversations, unexpected sights, a sudden desire one morning not to get into the saddle—all can be handled easily when one doesn't have to worry about getting somewhere by a certain time. And that's travel at its best.

After the *kind* of ride is decided, and assuming that one has determined a destination of some sort, one must choose a route. I employ a series of maps for this purpose, always working inward toward greater detail. That is, for a multistate tour I begin with a national map; for shorter rides, with a full state map; from these will come a very general orientation of population centers, rivers, mountain ranges. These maps (usually available free of charge from each state's department of transportation; obtain addresses from long-distance operator or the many sources listed below) are the service-station variety, "flat" maps that sometimes shade mountain ranges but provide no information of elevation gain or loss elsewhere. When hills require only an increased depression of the gas pedal, such information is unnecessary. But cyclists have a critical need for this knowledge. Not only will it affect one's training and later performance, but it will force one to take into account reduced daily mileages when computing the general time allotment for traveling through a region—and, therefore, one's financial outlay.

My next step is to consult a library's (or buy my own) "topographic" maps. As opposed to "flat" maps, these beauties indicate elevation gain or loss through the use of "contour lines." The theory is simple, and in half an hour a neophyte can be reading topos like a pro. At the bottom of each map is a "contour interval" designation of so many feet. The large-scale, single-state maps (1:500,000 scale; one inch equals eight miles) have an interval of five hundred feet. That is, every time a contour line is encountered along your route you will be gaining or losing five hundred feet of elevation (occasional figures on these lines tell you whether that's up- or downhill). If your path is free of these lines, you're pedaling the plains. If half a dozen exist in close proximity, you know you're pulling a mountain pass.

These single-state 1:500,000 scale topos are the first maps I consult after my initial work with the "flat" maps is completed. And sometimes I stop here, so that I'll be surprised by all the 499 foothills that don't show up. However, if I'm a bit pressed for road time and need to know more clearly what to expect, I move on to the next topos of greater detail—1:250,000 (one inch equals four miles). These have a contour interval of only two hundred feet, meaning of course that at a glance one can see rolling or hilly terrain.

One last scale, which I use most often for two-day dirt-road mountain-bike tours and when developing commuting routes in new cities, is the extremely detailed "7.5 minute" maps—on a 1:24,000 scale (one inch equals two thousand feet; contour interval of between ten and forty feet). These are in-

1:500,000 scale
1" = 8 miles
contour interval 500'

1:62,500 scale
1" = 1 mile
contour level 80'

Topo maps (both show the same area—the wonderful mountain bike ride of the White Rim Trail, at the confluence of the Green and Colorado Rivers in southern Utah).

valuable to backpackers and mountain bikers alike when reconnoitering in the woods. (Some cyclists swear by large-scale, cumbersome "county" maps. But these are "flat," expensive, and cover far too small an area for my taste.)

However, there's a catch with topos. Unlike most "flat" maps, which come folded nicely for the glove box, topos are huge. I normally buy a state base (1:500,000 scale) map for a ride, but these are several feet square. I've tried rolling them, folding them, even mailing them to myself along the trail. (A real pain, as my path often changes with local suggestions.) Finally, however, I came up with a system that works, and that doesn't require purchasing new maps all the time. The solution was to cut these maps into 7-by-10-inch sections (first indexing the sides of each section with A, B, C, or D, so as to fit them together again quickly and correctly), then photocopying them on regular 8½-by-11-inch paper (the wide border allows me to write in information gleaned from the more detailed scales). Sometimes on these copies I highlight rivers in blue, my intended route in red. Originals remain at home; the photocopied sheets can be folded one by one into the handlebar map case, consulted when necessary, and then discarded as the trip progresses.

Besides elevation, topographic maps provide detailed road classifications. Different colorings or markings indicate the categories of heavy-duty, medium-duty, light-duty, unimproved dirt roads, and interstate, U.S., and state highways. Map symbols include everything from footbridges and overpasses to dams and canals. Various shadings indicate swamps, wooded marshes, vineyards, orchards, and more. If your route takes you past a glacier, your topo map will show you the best way around it.

I've known some people to be put off by these wonderful maps, however, when at first glance they see only a scribbled mass of contour lines and road colors. It will be confusing, for about ten minutes. Then, if you're concentrating, the land will begin to take shape before your eyes. I first encountered topos in a ninth-grade science class, and recall the teacher's requiring us to use a magnifying glass to follow a river valley. It wasn't long before I was transfixed, seeing steep-walled canyons and level meadows come to life. Like those who hear music from written notes, cyclists can traverse a land even before their travel begins.

Major universities and public libraries often carry topos, as do many sports and specialty outdoor shops. If these sources turn up dry, write to the following addresses:

For areas east of the Mississippi River, including Minnesota, Puerto Rico, and the Virgin Islands:

> U.S. Geological Survey
> 1200 South Eads Avenue
> Arlington, VA 22202

For areas west of the Mississippi River, including Alaska, Hawaii, Louisiana, American Somoa, and Guam:

> U.S. Geological Survey
> P.O. Box 25286
> Federal Center
> Denver, CO 80225

Write first for an index, a price list, and a copy of the booklet *Topographic Maps*. It will take some of the mystery out of contour lines and symbols.

I suggest you pick up a "planimeter" (sometimes called simply a "map measurer") to aid in determining distances, as the usual city-to-city mileages provided by most maps are seldom computed along the secondary and back roads preferred by cyclists. This ingenious, inexpensive device has a tiny metal wheel that you roll along the map; a needle and gauge compute the inches traveled, and you multiply this by whatever scale map you're using. Presto— you have your mileage.

By the way, when determining your path, remember that most states bar bicycles from interstate highways when there is an "alternate road nearby." Unfortunately, "nearby" is seldom spelled out, and you can be hassled by police if your interpretation and his are different. I like the wide shoulders of most interstates, but wouldn't begin to purchase them at the cost of high-speed traffic noise. Unless there is no alternative, therefore, I avoid those routes and also the traffic-laden federal ("US"-designated) highways near population centers. You will be climbing more, and winding about, but back roads and state highways make for much better cycling.

Now you have a route, its distance, and its topography. But what of the weather? prevailing winds? local sights of scenic or historical importance? My next step is to write to a state's "office of tourism" or "travel council"; phone numbers and addresses can be obtained from long-distance operators, from the phone books of major cities nationwide carried in many libraries, and from cycle touring organizations and automobile clubs. In a short form letter, explain your intention of riding a particular route and request maps/road/weather information. Ask also about any laws concerning cyclists, and request the addresses of chambers of commerce in cities and large towns along your path. I know it sounds time-consuming, but a two-paragraph form letter is all you need. Keeping a copy of it will speed things up next year.

I am always extremely pleased with the quantity of information I receive and how quickly it usually arrives. These offices of course exist to facilitate tourists, but I've seen many peoples' protective instincts blossom when they read letters from a cyclist. Many times over the years I have received personal letters of encouragement and caution (always about traffic), plus suggested addresses for further information.

As with the map work, where I begin at a national or complete state level and work toward greater detail, I move from state offices of information to local chambers of commerce. From these I request their usual visitor information packet, plus data on weather, local bike clubs, roads, and hostels (inexpensive, overnight accommodations).

Concerning weather, most states provide an annual overview that I find sufficient, given my personal dictum of "Go prepared for anything, and then enjoy it all." Your local library will carry desk reference national atlases with

While almost any compass will do for pavement touring, I like something more professional—like this Brunton model—for back roads and trail riding.

maximum/minimum/monthly average temperatures, plus monthly precipitation levels. These are great for general, overall tour-planning, as one can choose a period that usually (read *not always*) has moderate heat and little rain. But such information can lull you into trouble, when a cold snap has you shivering in a wet, early-morning ride.

Information on prevailing winds is crucial *if* they are strong and relatively constant during a particular time of year. You will be warned—sometimes—by local or state offices, and always by fellow cyclists when you write to bike shops or clubs. Another source of very general wind information is *The National Atlas of the United States of America;* winds during all four seasons are computed and shown in direction, speed, and constancy on four seasonal, national maps. I've written elsewhere that simple acceptance of head winds is the best answer to these troubling, unseen foes, that wind is part of the package a biker bites off when he chooses his mode of travel. I face them when I have to, and persevere. But I *always* try to plan around them.

By this time you'll have a good deal of information, but much more is available with just a bit more effort. For example, if you belong to the American Automobile Association, or know someone who does, you have a wealth of wonderful data at your fingertips. (So much, in fact, that even when I didn't own a car I maintained my membership.) Not only maps and campground guides, but the excellent TourBooks on every state come your way. These provide historical and geographical overviews of states and individual towns and cities, descriptions of national parks and monuments, museum displays, addresses of important state offices, maps of urban centers, motels costs and phone numbers, and much more.

Detailed route information from fellow cyclists is available from Bikecentennial (which bills itself as "The Bicycle Travel Association"; this address and others in appendix), and also from the oldest of this country's bike organizations, The League of American Wheelmen, which was founded in 1880. Most commonly referred to simply as the "LAW" (with each letter pronounced, not spoken as a single word), and more lately as "Bicycle USA," their annual *Bicycle USA Almanac* is, I think, the best single informational journal for touring cyclists. Updated each year, the *Almanac* contains a "Touring Information Request" form, and for each state the address and phone number of a "Touring Information Director," addresses of local bike clubs and state tourist information offices, specific bike maps/books available, notes on the year-round climate, and the address for the national "Hospitality Home List." This last item is available only to LAW members, and by itself is worth the moderate annual club fee, for the names listed are of those people across the nation who have opened their homes to touring cyclists. Membership costs less than a single night in a motel, but this is the least of what I've gained from most such layovers. Nothing can beat the feeling of pedaling into town as a stranger, and leaving as a friend.

Yet another source of route information, though most often looked to simply for their 250-odd inexpensive, overnight lodgings and the one-day and weekend rides organized by local chapters, is American Youth Hostels (AYH). I have stayed in hostels across the states, next to St. Peter's in London, in the shadow of an Austrian castle, on an island in the Nile, in Jerusalem—the list goes on. And so do the memories of coming off solo rides to enjoy the camaraderie of fellow travelers.

I have mentioned several times throughout this book a suggestion that cycle touring is preeminently suited for escaping the normal world of disciplined time. It is during this critical phase of the tour—the planning phase—that "clock consciousness" is engineered into or out of a ride.

For example, we'll assume that in training rides with full gear you and your group have determined a physical ability to pedal seventy miles per day. Having looked at the area on topo maps you've trained in similar country, and know you can average approximately ten to twelve miles per hour (pretty standard, I'd say, even with a five- or ten-minute break each hour). That is only seven hours in the saddle out of each twenty-four, which makes it seem extremely easy to clip off the seventy mpd.

You have two weeks' vacation. From those fourteen days we'll subtract two days' travel time, which leaves us with twelve. Subtract two more days for times you might wish to sightsee entirely on foot—in an urban center, perhaps, or for short hikes in the hills, or simply for some lounging about a mountain town or seashore. Now we're down to ten days: multiplied by seventy mpd it gives an impressive total of seven hundred miles.

Now you can fine-tune your planning, for a large round-trip of that distance (especially convenient when a car is driven to the take-off point), or a one-way seven-hundred-mile ride.

Or can you? Most of us have work schedules that preclude more than a weekend of touring during training, meaning only two back-to-back seventy mile days. There is always the chance that you, or someone in your party, will find that riding such a distance consistently is less pleasurable than expected. If you've planned a round-trip, such a development is not fatal; you can simply begin your turn homeward a bit earlier. But what if you have plane tickets home from a destination seven hundred miles away? In that case, despite your riding preference (or sudden desire to dawdle in interesting places along the way), you must stick with the original mpd schedule.

My guess is that you'll have little trouble, ultimately, in determining your own physical ability for saddle time—*if* you've trained. And if you've trained *as a group* for a group ride, this might not be a problem. It is instead the social aspects of a tour that most often wreak havoc, when individual desires for more time spent out of the saddle begin unraveling the earlier group-determined schedule. For these reasons I suggest you ride only with people you know very, very well.

Beyond the considerations above, planning a tour becomes as personal as one's delights in travel. I mentioned earlier my preference for riding along historic trails—spending evenings in my tent reading explorer or pioneer journals, imagining the land as it was then, attempting to understand the changes in intervening centuries, passing hours discussing local history with café mates and those who live along the trail. Fortunately, almost all parts of our nation are laced with such trails; a good library will have maps of explorations, pioneer routes, Indian paths, military marches. I've followed Lewis and Clark, Dominguez and Escalanate, Coronado, Pike, Pony Express, Gila, Sherman (in his march to the sea), Hole-in-the-Rock, part of the Oregon, Donner, and Mormon trails, and more. And many remain.

Let racers concentrate on their pulse rates and pedal rpm; tourers—especially those following historic trails, or noting the natural history of the region they're pedaling, or simply going slow enough to see the land about them—will instead discover that amazingly rich and interesting world *outside* themselves.

8

Lodging

THE FOLLOWING QUESTION comes my way often at the end of cycle touring slide shows, and appears to rank as a major concern just behind the two primary fears of physical ability and bicycle repair: "But where do you sleep?" I've gone into this a bit in the last chapter, and suggested some literature that provides information on motels, campgrounds, and hostels. Yet most of my nights, and many of my most memorable ones, have been spent in settings other than these. This short chapter is therefore designed to ease your fears about where to sleep, no matter where you find yourself at dusk.

I established earlier my reason for packing along at least a minimum of sleeping gear—the increased freedom that comes from not having to reach one's motel reservations every day. For warm-weather rides this gear can be a shelter as simple and lightweight as a one-pound bivy sack. The warmth of insulated underwear, plus the warmth provided by the bivy, takes the place of a sleeping bag. Cold-weather touring, of course, requires additional gear, and thus on shorter tours (especially weekenders) most cyclists prefer to avoid the additional weight by cutting back their mileages and staying inside. Decreasing daily mileages reduces the anxiety of reaching each day's destination, and allows for the spontaneity so often missing in "scheduled-stop" rides.

Many people have the impression that when cyclists decide against a motels-only tour they are required to travel with all the gear requirements of campers. Perish the thought. I've never done what is today termed "family camping," but I see it when sharing an occasional campsite or evening meal with these people. I would no doubt pack just as much into the woods if I had the room for doing so (I've noticed that whatever is the size of my pannier system, I always fill it), but motor-home (or even station wagon) and cycle camping lie at opposite extremes in the need for accountrements. Perhaps a clearer idea of how many cyclists "camp" is conveyed by the phrase "sleeping in the woods" (or prairie, mountains, at the beach, or wherever). I might go so far as to build a campfire, after rolling out my bag and tent or bivy. But most often I simply set up my bedding, eat a cold meal (if I haven't already had dinner in the last small town, or plan to heat up dehydrated soup in winter), and, with the aid of the fire or my trusty candle lantern, read into the night.

The gear requirements are minimal. But *where* does one sleep?

First, realize that your anxiety is natural. After all, how many times during one's life is such a question present? Perhaps while on vacation, or on a long drive. But then you're in a car, which at least allows relatively quick access to the next town down the road. Again, the anxiety is natural; don't waste time berating yourself for it. It's dusk, you're on a bike, there's no campground near, you're alone. That can be a scary set of circumstances, especially if you haven't thought about it beforehand.

The second step, therefore, is to have thought about the situation before it takes place—the reason for this chapter—and thus to begin looking for a good place to sleep *before* it's dusk. My worst nights have been spent when I didn't follow this advice. (Such as the time my buddy and I dawdled in downtown Budapest, not having the money to rent a room and not knowing how long it would take us to reach the countryside. We ended up pitching our tent between ramshackle buildings next to the railroad tracks, and we spent the night wondering when the police would arrive, demanding our passports.)

Now, if you're pedaling along National Forest or BLM (Bureau of Land Management) land, all you really need concern yourself with is choosing a good patch of ground. This is because camping anywhere in such areas is usually permitted. In much of the West, where relatively huge amounts of land are owned by the federal government, one often needs simply to determine you're not on a bombing range, and bed down. Good maps will provide this information, and signs usually indicate if camping is permitted only in designated spots. Most of the time, when riding along such federal holdings, I merely distance myself from the road a half hour before nightfall and roll out my bag. (Unless, that is, I'm in bear country. Then I choose a tree some distance from my camp and suspend my food, looping my parachute cord over a branch so that the saddlebag with all the food is about twelve feet above the ground to keep it out of the bear's reach. *Don't* keep it, or any clothing with the smell of food, in the tent with you.)

Some books on backpacking deal at length with the topic of choosing a proper campsite. They examine it in time-consuming, almost Zen-like, detail, which they also apply to such herculean tasks as "preparing breakfast" and "foot care." I've never understood this preoccupation with the mundane. A touring cyclist's foot care is clean socks and good shoes; his breakfast, either purchased in a café or instant oats over the fire. And choosing a campsite in the woods? It's simple. Avoid anthills, and don't sleep in drainages.

I'm serious. What, after all, are the requirements for a good sleep? Comfort is first—which we've covered already in our discussion of equipment. This is also where drainages come in, avoiding creek beds and low river banks so that you won't wake up wet. Next in necessity is an undisturbed sleep, obtained by camping some distance from the road, and either choosing a tent of subdued colors or erecting it behind trees or rocks. I make it a practice not to sleep at roadside parks, or anywhere that a passing motorist's headlights will strike me. In this way the first thing to disturb me will be the rising sun.

We're still on the second step of determining where to sleep. (First came understanding one's natural anxiety; second is beginning one's search before dusk and knowing what to look for.) Once you begin looking at sleep-options in the simple terms of comfort and remaining undisturbed, an amazing array of alternatives will present themselves. In roughly the same category as the federal lands mentioned are state-administered holdings, again determined through map work and your "planning phase" pre-trip letters. Then there are the millions of private farms with wooded or prairie lands, and ranches out West with free desert scrub by the square mile.

I said before that I've almost never been turned down when asking permission to sleep on someone's land. This goes not only for rural settings, but in urban areas as well. The trick is to choose carefully and to be attentive to those factors that make someone willing to share their land, barn, garage, or basement.

First, there's your personal appearance and demeanor. By this I don't mean a short haircut and hat-doffing, suppliant stance. I'm referring instead to looking like a person who is actually doing what you say—touring by bicycle. If I'm not noticed (usually by the farm dog) as I pedal up the drive, I always attempt to position my bicycle so that it can be seen from the door. In this manner I'm more easily believed by whoever answers my knock.

In mentioning demeanor I'm referring to something I've seen only rarely in regard to finding accommodations, but far more often concerning riding habits in traffic. This is the somewhat haughty air that a few cyclists possess, apparent in those who feel superior to motorists (either physically or environmentally), and thus take up more road space than is required. And it is apparent too when groups (usually) of riders invade a small town or geographic region (like the cyclist-inundated San Juan Islands near Seattle) and foist upon the occupants the problem of where to sleep. You may have fought head winds all day long, at last reached civilization, and enjoyed a café meal, and now find that it is too dark to ride safely out of town. Of course you didn't plan it that way. Nevertheless, that doesn't make it the responsibility of some small-town sheriff to overlook the rules against camping in the city park.

In choosing the place where I'll ask permission to spend the night I look for those attributes that will make it easy for the owner to say yes, such as a large lot (if near a town); a larger—rather than smaller—farm, with sufficient land or a barn where I won't have to sleep too near the farmhouse; a place where a man is present (it's to be expected that a woman might take pause at letting a windblown male rider spend the night, though this has very seldom been the case when my bike is within sight). I normally look over the spot from the road, and when introducing myself and asking permission to stay *I* suggest a campsite, and mention that I of course won't be building a fire, will be pushing on early in the morning, and so forth. With just a bit of practice you'll become as good as a salesman at recognizing who needs such assurances. Very often—especially when I'm touring with a woman—people are quick to suggest a more comfortable alternative than the spot I've suggested. (Female tourers tell me they have little trouble in obtaining permission to camp, and often benefit from a "protective" or overly helpful response from men and women alike.)

Don't try your luck too near an inexpensive motel or campground, and be as creative in your requests as you were in route planning. Jails, for instance, have been very handy during my travels. I've stayed in some two dozen jails across the country, for some of the most interesting nights of my life. When I was sixteen, for instance, my fifteen-year-old buddy and I found ourselves in downtown Marinette, Wisconsin, on a windswept summer evening. Riding without a tent on that trip, we pedaled to the jail and requested a cell for the night. The male jail was full, and we found ourselves being driven in a squad car to the female pen, then marched down a long hall of cells full of hard-looking women. At last locked up, we heard the two women next to us ask the guard as he walked past, "What did they do?" The guard grunted a terse, convincing reply, "Shot a gas station attendant."

Several hours of questions began, directed at us by these women we couldn't see, then passed by them from cell to cell. "Why'd you shoot him?" we were asked. And suppressing our laughter we'd deepen our voices and respond, "Cause we felt like it." What an evening!

Your public library will contain many national campground guides (the appropriate pages of which can be photocopied for the trail), and the sources mentioned in the previous chapter and listed in the appendix should provide you with plenty of options as to where to sleep. But it is these chance happenings—the jail stays and conversations with prisoners, a night spent in a Canadian warehouse and rounds walked with the Indian watchman, a barn in New Mexico where I was trapped by an angry bull for half an hour the following morning—that are so much sweeter.

I have met a few riders who pack no shelter whatsoever, thereby forcing themselves to seek out such experiences. As with most things in cycle touring I prefer having a choice, and imagine most of you will also choose to pack at least those two lightest of shelters—a bivy and a VISA card. Just don't fall into the constant habit of motels or campground only. The world's far too diverse for that.

9

All-terrain Touring

In the past chapters I've talked often of the pleasure in meeting people along the trail. Every now and then, however, I want to be *alone*. The craving for distance from the sounds of cars, their occupants, the civilized world in general, is at times common to us all.

Many people have satisfied this urge through backpacking. I apologize if you've found offensive my earlier tongue-in-cheek swipes at this activity; they are made with full knowledge that all sports are not for all people. As I've said, I come honestly to my difficulties. I got out of the army as this craze was at its zenith; the last thing I wanted on my back was a pack. Perhaps it is a comment on my mental limitations, but I find the all-day plodding about beneath such weight to be boring, except in the most spectacular and varied surroundings. My final—and greatest—problem is that, except for extensive travel through remote wilderness, I find a far more comfortable alternative in my much preferred mountain-bike/day-hike approach.

I've found few areas that aren't amenable to such a pleasant assault. By car I cover the distance between home and the end of asphalt or two-wheel-drive dirt road. Loading my bike (with far more gear than I could cram into a single pack) I then clip off the four-wheel drive dirt road miles to where the

Right: Art Edison on a one-day winter ride.

trail begins. *Walking* my bike—if it's a wilderness area—along the trail a few miles comes next, until I find a good spot for a base camp. And last are the relatively uninhibited (lightweight waist or daypack only) day hikes from camp.

Far more often, however, I simply choose remote two- or four-wheel-drive roads that run through the areas I want to visit. The attraction is usually a combination of scenery and the fun of riding, sometimes a site too distant for hiking and approachable only by jeep, horse, noisy motorcycle, or silent mountain bike. ATBs can be expensive, but they're a steal compared to cars and hayburners.

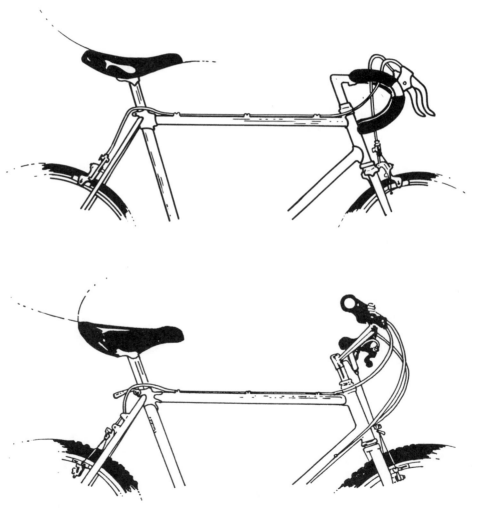

Mountain bike profile showing upright bars, cantilever brakes, quick-release seatpost, and knobby tires.

ATB strapless toe clip; notice also the pedal reflector (these should be present front and rear), pants clips, and abrasions on outside of pedal.

I mentioned earlier what wonderful commuting vehicles mountain bikes can be, how their inherent stability and amazing maneuverability make them perfect for the urban-jungle ride to work. It doesn't take much imagination to see the possibilities for these machines in the countryside, for making ATBs the health-providing vehicle encouraging the pursuit of other hobbies. (I've equipped mine, for instance, with special camera bags and tripod holders, rigged it for trout fishing, packed out deer lashed to the handlebars and draped across the saddle.) And from earlier chapters you already know sufficient basics in frame design, composition, componentry, training, and planning a ride to steer you well into the purchase of a mountain bike and execution of an all-terrain tour. What remains are the minor, necessary additions to the mechanical side of ATBs, a further note on training, water purification, and, finally, a warning against the illegal use of mountain bikes in the wild.

PARTICULARS

Frames

I stated earlier, in the discussion of frame geometry, that ATBs traditionally have gentler, more shallow seat and head-tube angles than thin-tire touring bikes (to put the rider's weight over the rear tire, thus providing the greater traction necessary for steep climbs on unpaved surfaces). I also mentioned that this is changing somewhat, toward steeper angles for faster handling, requiring the rider to shift his weight backward in the saddle for uphill traction. I repeat these points so you will remember to test-ride several mountain bikes when shopping; don't assume they'll all feel the same. Frame geometry and composition (remember our short discussion earlier of metallurgy, of high tensile steel, chro-moly, aluminum) determine both the quickness and stiffness you may or may not prefer in your ride.

Bike fit is also different on an ATB, but once again—no matter what you hear elsewhere—there is not a single industry standard. Most shops will suggest a frame at least two inches smaller than your touring bike, some an even greater variance to allow for the different kind of riding.

However, I've found that relatively nonradical ATB riders (those who primarily commute and pedal dirt roads on tour) prefer larger frames overall than do those who are most attracted to the "skiing on wheels" sensation that mountain bikes can provide. There is an entire generation now which has grown up on BMX bikes; leaping logs and jumping rocks on ATBs for them seems the next logical step. For the rest of us, however, that would be an *unsafe* step, at

ATB profile. Notice: larger diameter tubing, upright handlebars, wheels smaller in diameter but much heavier and wider, oversize fenders, shorter wheelbase, wider (bear trap) pedals, and quick-release seatpost lever.

least until we've learned the techniques required. Again, test-ride several bikes before you make a decision. (My ATBs are roughly two inches smaller than my thin-tire frames; if the majority of my riding was on trails I'd opt for a four-inch difference.)

Handlebars

It's great to be able to steer, shift, and apply the brakes without moving one's hands from the bars. A necessity when off-road and on four-wheel-drive dirt roads, it's also an extremely safe and convenient attribute for big-city riding. All ATBs have the brakes and gear-shift levers where they can be controlled from the bars, but not all handlebars are the same. Some are almost perfectly straight, some slightly swept back toward the rider, and some of late are pulled back even more from the ends. Be sure to position yourself correctly in regard to top tube length and saddle placement, and *then* decide which bar style you prefer.

ATB handlebar closeup showing foam grips, thumb-operated shifters, motorcycle-style brake handles, fingerbell, and high-rise stem.

Brakes

Cantilevers were once the name of the game on mountain bikes (and are still preferred by many on the front wheel). Then came "roller cams," and problems. In a word—one that has been heard in many bike shops—they're "finicky." More powerful, surely, and wonderfully smooth, but only when clean and adjusted properly. Adjustments are tricky on these things, and who ever heard of keeping mud and snow away from the brakes of a mountain bike, especially when roller cams are fitted so close over the wheel? (Which, by the way, makes it extremely difficult to mount fenders. And when fenders are at last wedged beneath them and into place over the tire, the reduced clearance makes mud- and snow-jamming a real problem. I've been forced on tour to remove fenders just to be able to continue pushing my bike, and then only with repeated cleanings of debris from the brake/tire junctions. Speaking of fenders, you'll find two major brands available, in different lengths and widths. The longest, widest—and unfortunately, therefore, the heaviest—provide greatest protection. Hoping to avoid this weight, and the problem of attachment time and crud buildup beneath the fender, I tested a rear rack top-mounted plastic guard, and a down-tube mounted shield; both are offered as protection from the muck thrown up from rear tire on the back, and front tire onto the feet, legs, and front. Let me say only that I wasted a clean set of clothes, and about ten bucks, in learning that these do a better job than no fender at all, but not nearly good enough.)

A few answers to these brake headaches have surfaced. One is a power cam model that is easier to adjust but just as powerful. Another is the simple, inexpensive cordura "roller cam cover" made by some pannier companies. And a final option is the U-brake.*

One last consideration. Female readers especially should check out their ability to span the brake lever distance from the bar. Small hands often find this difficult, but various "reaches" are available (some brakes even have an adjustable "lever-reach").

Bottom bracket

Compare the heights of these between bikes, especially if you think you'll be doing a fair amount of trail riding. The higher the bracket the larger the log or rock you can clear without contact.

Remember bracket height if you decide to buy a kickstand (extremely useful for commuting, but also in touring when you want to leave your bike

*NOTE: Roller cams and U-brakes which are found beneath the chainstays offer no difficulties whatsoever to the mounting of fenders. Also, the regular plate (shaped somewhat like a triangle; this is the piece reaching down toward the tire) on roller cam brakes can be hacksawed to increase tire clearance—thereby attaining very easy fender placement.

upright and haven't a tree or wall nearby). Longer stands are now available, and can be trimmed to perfect fit.

Mirror

Most of my all-terrain rides are truly all-terrain—some pavement, a lot of dirt-road miles, a bit of trail (or a lot of this last type of travel, when it's legal). For this purpose I prefer to ride with a mirror. Check out the Rhode Gear "Cycle Mirror"—attached in a snap with velcro strap. I don't like to have to wrap my hand around its mount, but it's the best I've seen thus far.

Gearing

I suggested earlier a thin-tire gear range of mid-twenties to slightly more than one hundred. But the conditions of much steeper unpaved hills and the difficulty of traction make an even lower gear attractive on an ATB (I've recently switched to an inside chainring of only twenty-four teeth, which when combined with my largest freewheel cog of thirty provides a *very* low 20.8 inch gear). Many mountain bikes come standard with a highest gear of only eighty-five (produced most often by a forty-six-tooth chainring and a fourteen-tooth smallest freewheel cog), which for me just isn't high enough to take advantage of down hills, tail winds, good spirits, or paved roads. I boost my high end by dropping the smallest cog to a thirteen and increasing the largest chainring to a forty-eight.

Tires

When the standard twenty-six-inch-diameter mountain-bike tires first appeared, they were huge (2.125″ in width), soft (35–40 psi), and extremely slow (full knobby tread). Many kinds are now available, from narrow "street" tires without knobs, to "combinations" for multiterrain use, to somewhat lighter skinwall full knobbies (best for traction in loose terrain and mud, snow, and sand). By far my preferences for all-around touring are the "combinations" that are relatively wide, of skinwall construction, and knobbed in such a manner that on pavement they ride on a near-constant bead of rubber, thus avoiding the staccato "bumping" of knobs on hard surfaces. Two such tires are the excellent, variable-pressure (40–80 psi) Specialized Crossroads II (1.95″ wide), and the Ritchey "Quad" (1.9″ wide). As with everything in biking, know your options before you buy. Most shops will give you a few bucks off stock tires if you want to swap original equipment, but only at the time of bike purchase.

Racks

My personal preference, as with thin-tire bikes, is for the chro-moly beauties by Bruce Gordon. Remember, when looking around, that ATB racks must take a

*ATB tire-tread pattern which
allows a smooth ride on pavement
due to interlinking knobs.*

great deal more abuse, and think also about how the rack will fit with cantilever, roller cam, or U-brake, and whether mounting brackets will handle the larger frame tubes.

But one warning in particular: Avoid low-riders on mountain bikes. Fall into a deep rut and you'll end up knocking off your front panniers; try to wind through brush, cactus, or high rocks and you'll bang up your bags. Front low-riders on ATBs just don't make sense, as the shorter, wider wheels and tires of mountain bikes, and their heavy-duty frames make them so stable that the slight amount gained by low-riders fails to offset problems.

Panniers

Many companies now put out saddlebags designed specifically for mountain bikes, with heavier-weight cordura to handle the increased abrasions and more secure mounting techniques to enable bags to remain in place no matter how the bike is bounced about. Lone Peak sports an easily accessible "Lock-On" system; Kirtland offers a behind-the-back "Lever-Loc"; Robert Beckman Designs employs a strap system (which is very easy to reach and pull tight, yet locks the pannier to the rack as if it were glued into place, whatever the terrain) identical to that used in their thin-tire models; buy one set of Beckmans and you're set for life with both kinds of bikes. Other companies have already developed or are at present developing attachment systems to handle trails, so shop carefully.

*Right: Glacier Park ranger Lynn Emerick with bike loaded for a
weekend of daytime photography and lodges at night.*

One huge consideration for anyone buying panniers is, of course, cost. And this is doubled when one considers packs for both thin- and fat-tire touring rigs. Keep this in mind when shopping for bags, as you'll find several mountain lines that can be used well on pavement, but few thin-tire packs that will stay on off-road.

Review the earlier discussion of panniers for general comments, but let me remind you of one point now. If you plan to tour with tent, sleeping bag, and ground pad loaded perpendicularly to the rear rack (thus hanging over the top of the panniers on either side), do *not* choose top-loading bags. They're fine in front, where one seldom carries anything wide across the rack. But in back they make access to the bag's contents extremely difficult.

Water purification

Don't forget my earlier warnings about the amazing quantity of water a rider requires, and the difficulties posed by that backcountry bane, Giardia. Remember: Purification tablets will not kill it. Furious boiling or filtration is required, and of these the second choice is greatly preferable. I pack along the "First-Need" purifier, which I've found to be fast, reliable, and relatively inexpensive.

TRAINING

Load up and ride a rough four-wheel-drive road or trail, and you'll learn the same lesson that came my way a few years ago: All-terrain touring requires far more upper-torso strength than does riding a thin-tire bike.

I mentioned earlier my attempts to gain it—plus aerobic and anaerobic fitness—through jogging, riding, weight lifting, and rowing. The problem was the time required to do all these things. At last I found a shortcut answer to the power *and* endurance my riding required, through the Schwinn Air-Dyne.

Now, this is not a product endorsement, beyond the fact that *for me* the solution is an exercycle that taxes both lower and upper torsos, and at present I don't know of any machine except the Air-Dyne that does this. The control panel of digital clock/odometer/rpm speedometer/ergometer tells me precisely how much (or how little) I'm doing, and is perfect for the timed, measured-work-load, thirty-second bursts I make for power.

Remember that this is simply my personal, preferred training. You might find a gym-class-type routine of pushups and pullups sufficient.

WHERE TO RIDE

I dealt with this topic in an earlier book *(The Mountain Bike Manual),* and I have received kind words from both park rangers and mountain bikers on my treatment of this sticky issue. As the battle lines have remained essentially unchanged, I've borrowed from my earlier discussion:

> In February of 1984, while cycling across the Southwest, I took a long side trip to view the cliff dwellings in the Gila National Forest. In conversation with rangers there I learned that a large group of mountain bikers had appeared several weeks before, determined to ride the trails through the adjoining wilderness area. They were informed that such travel is illegal in:
>
> a) *wilderness areas:* means of "mechanical transport" in such areas is disallowed by the Wilderness Act of 1964;
> b) *national parks:* except on roads, and those paths specifically marked "bike path";
> c) *national forests:* except on roads and in those areas specified for "multiple use";
> d) *national monuments:* except on roads open to the public;
> e) *most state parks and monuments:* except on roads and paths specifically marked "bike path."

(Now, don't get upset; there are plenty of places left to ride and we'll get to them shortly.)

The rangers told me that some of the bikers became indignant. "We don't do as much damage as horses!" one cried, and several spoke of their "right" to ride the trails. Another biker said he had heard of a recent change in the ruling, but the ranger was ready with a reply. Apparently this rumor of a change was widespread, and brought the following clarification:

> A bicycle is a form of mechanical transport the use of which is prohibited in wilderness by Section 4 (c) of the Wilderness Act and Title 36 CFR 293.6. The fact that the "enforcement regulation" was moved from the status of a mandatory regulation in Subpart A of CFR 261 to a discretionary regulation in Subpart B did not make bicycling a legal use within wilderness. It simply gave Supervisors discretion on how they approach the problem—by education and discouragement of occasional use, or by use of a law enforcement punishment approach through CFR 261.

In short, the action was still illegal. Only the park supervisor's *reaction* had been made discretionary.

So the law is clear. But should it be changed? After all, the Wilderness Act was passed long before mountain bikes were on the scene. And what of the issue of the comparative damage done by horses? And the more sticky problem of one's "right" to use a trail?

The National Off Road Bicycle Association (NORBA) has tried to gain access to wilderness trails. They approached the Sierra Club in hope of support for their lobbying efforts, but were rebuffed. The reasons given by the Sierra Club are interesting, and center around trail damage: soil erosion and deep tire ruts on steep portions of the paths, and new tracks made between turns when mountain bikers couldn't follow the switchbacks. Park rangers have told me of their fear for the "fragile ecosystems" easily damaged by bikers who ride the trails for the thrills involved in fast turns, sharp climbs, and breakneck speed descents. They argue that horses generally remain on the paths and travel at a leisurely pace, neither of which is true for many mountain bikes. "Most people agree that motorized dirt bikes should be kept off the trails," a ranger told me at California's Anza-Borrego Desert State Park. "Well," she continued, "there's not much difference in the damage done by one of them and by ten mountain bikes."

But beyond ruts and soil erosion is the effect produced merely by the appearance of a bike in the wilderness. On many occasions—while hiking in the Wind Rivers, ski touring in Utah, and squirrel hunting in the deep woods of Missouri—I've quietly cursed the jet flying silently overhead. Though unheard and having no impact upon the trail, I perceive these mechanical devices as intruders. In this day of man's increasingly mechanical approach to the outdoors, when thousands experience nature not for what it is through observation but as a playground, there aren't many places left where one is guaranteed one won't be run over by a jeep or snowmobile or mountain bike. Preserving those areas—at the cost of a disgruntled few—seems worth the price.

Cycle magazines do little to assist the off-road bikers' image with the public when they publish such articles as "Log Jumping for Trail Riders" (*Bicycling*, June 1984). This piece is illustrated with "six distinct steps in a log crossing," with the combatants pictured in full color. The moss-covered log is a lovely medley of dappled browns and greens, a forest behemoth surrounded by its fellow trees and lime-colored ferns. In the other corner is the biker, dressed in helmet, gloves, blue skin suit, and knee and shin pads—looking more prepared for a moon shot than for a ride in the countryside.

In the article we are warned that if our ATB has large chainrings we should take them off, lest we "wreck them." Nothing is said about the damage done to the "recreational" log while we're wrecking our chainrings on it, or the damage done in dragging a lubricated chain across the moss. Granted, the forest area pictured is no doubt "legal" for mountain bikes. And it may even be just a small wooded piece of land on the edge of a subdivision. But other visitors—in any area—should be able to rest themselves without fear of getting grease on their pants.

If the author is successful, if he does "teach" us to look at "logs, rocks, and other large objects" differently, where will it end? What happens when, for "fun," they're all viewed as obstacles and race courses, when forests, prairies, and mountains are turned into amusement parks? "Cycling" was synonymous with "low impact," "environmentally pure," and "socially conscious." Once touted as a "pollution solution" and an "answer to the Arabs," those days of delicate hopes seem to have gone the way of oil embargoes. But both will be back. Meanwhile, hikers, thoughtful bikers, and the public will begin considering the ban of mountain bikes from *all* lands. What a shame!

So much for where you *can't* ride. Your bike shop dealer will probably know of those nearby national and state parks and forests which—in addition to their "on-limits" roads—do have specific bike paths. And then there are the countless miles of paved and dirt roads, "multiple-use" forest land, backwoods lumber roads, and fire trails. Don't make yourself miserable by concentrating on the few areas that exclude mountain bikes, especially when it will take a lifetime to ride the areas that *are* open.

10

On-the-Road Repairs

WHAT A DISTASTEFUL topic! But before you shut the book and utter a silent prayer that you'll never have to lift a wrench to your machine, read the following few paragraphs. They are designed, first, to tell you not to feel alone in your dread of things mechanical, and second, to make you see that mechanics—at least on a bike—*can* be understood by the average human.

You might think by now that with all the miles I put on a bike each year I must love working on one. Dead wrong. I'm not blessed with an aptitude for mechanics; I haven't a gift for understanding how things work. And whereas I don't much mind the easily removed "natural" residue of a day's hard riding, I *hate* grease.

But what is a biker supposed to do, when he breaks down far from home? I've said before that working on one's bike is much like a trip to the dentist— disagreeable, but occasionally necessary.

Now let me give you the good news: Repairing a bicycle is a piece of cake, compared to most of what in life will trouble you mechanically.

Picture the bicycle. Two wheels, a frame, brakes, a transmission that is *completely* mechanical, and easy to get at. Of course, there are bearings hidden in the wheels and cables that run from handlebars to two derailleurs. But only those of us who are out for months at a time must worry themselves with bearings. And what's confusing about cables? It's like not understanding the essence of a clothesline.

Because bikes are solely mechanical (you can actually *see* what happens when you turn a screw), and the parts are easily accessible, you can learn enough of the basics to get by. Read the following repair procedures like normal prose and you'll think it's Greek. But take your time, step by step, with your bike before you, and it will all make sense.

TOOLS

Don't be put off by the drawing. I thought it best to include *all* the tools I use (some at home, some on the road) for doing every repair on my bike. Most cross-country tourers travel with far less than the list I provided in Chapter 2 (p. 53), and weekend travelers often manage with a kit of only allen wrenches, a six-inch crescent, a small screwdriver, tire irons, and a spare tube (and/or patch kit).

1. *Crescent wrench—15".* I far prefer a vise to pull my freewheel, but this does a good job of it and is far less expensive. When at home I use it in place of my "pocket vise," and instead of my six-inch crescent for pulling off a cotterless crank (the six-inch must be used when on the road, but the strain on this small tool is great).

2. *Crescent wrench—6".* The tool most used by touring cyclists. Be sure to buy quality; the slide mechanism on a cheap one will in time refuse to stay cinched tightly against a nut.

3. *Crescent wrench—4".* Very nice for brake work, if you don't plan to purchase a set of metric open or box ends. Remember that this tool, like so many others pictured, will not be carried on the road and isn't really necessary for home repair. It is included because it makes some jobs easier than do the larger wrenches.

4. *Channel locks—7".* This is an excellent road tool for tightening headsets, and for gripping anything too large for the six-inch crescent.

5. *Vise grips.* A large pair is required to remove blips from rim walls, something that, if you're lucky and also keep your tires properly inflated, you may never need to do.

6. *Regular blade screwdriver.* I pack a thin, lightweight, short-handled screwdriver, which, with long shank included, measures six inches in length; the flat blade tip (only 3/16" wide) is perfect for very fine adjustments of derailleur set screws. Buy a poor quality screwdriver and the blade will bend and chip in no time.

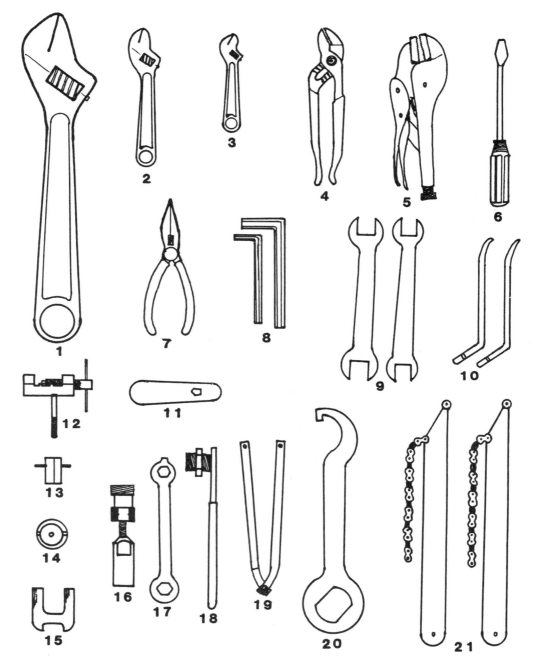

Tools.

1) crescent wrench—15"
2) crescent wrench—6"
3) crescent wrench—4"
4) channel locks—7"
5) vise grips
6) regular blade screwdriver
7) needle-nose pliers
8) allen wrenches
9) cone wrenches
10) tire levers
11) Swiss Army Knife
12) chain rivet tool
13) spoke nipple wrench
14) freewheel tool
15) pocket vise
16) cotterless crank removal tool
17) universal cotterless crank wrench
18) universal cotterless crankarm puller
19) universal adjustable cup tool
20) lock ring/fixed cup bottom bracket tool
21) freewheel sprocket tools

7. *Needle-nose pliers.* I prefer a small pair with side cutters (for trimming brake and gear cables).

8. *Allen wrenches.* Do not leave on a long ride without making sure you have an allen for each and every allen head on the bike, for the Fates will surely cause that single bolt you've overlooked to loosen up. Also, do not try to get by with an allen wrench that "almost" fits; you'll end up rounding off the corners and ruining the bolt.

9. *Cone wrenches.* Make sure they are thin and lightweight and that they fit your cones. Don't buy the far heavier shop models unless you plan never to pack these along on a ride.

10. *Tire levers.* I pack only two, for I find the third one sold in most sets to be unnecessary. The tips must be perfectly smooth, or you'll be puncturing your tube while trying to repair it.

11. *Swiss army knife.* Extremely handy for many reasons. I carry one primarily on long rides.

12. *Chain rivet tool.* Necessary for removing a chain, adding links, and freeing frozen links. Be sure the rivet tool you are buying will fit the chain on your bike.

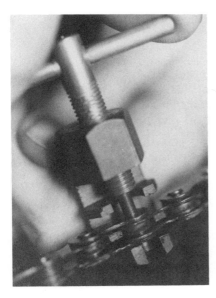

Chain rivet tool in action;
notice rivet pin being pushed
through the roller and side plate.

13. *Spoke nipple wrench.* The "T" type is pictured; this model, and the "hoop" style wrench, are my preferences over the round multisize nipple wrenches. Make sure the wrench you purchase will fit your spokes.

14. *Freewheel tool.* Most freewheels require removal tools specific to their brand. Match these up before hitting the road, for removal of the freewheel is necessary for spoke replacement on the freewheel side (a *very* infrequent repair).

*Freewheel tool (top),
pocket vise (bottom).*

15. *Pocket vise.* These wonderful creations are necessary—along with the freewheel tool above—for freewheel removal on the road. Large vises, or the fifteen-inch crescent wrench mentioned, are my preferences at home, but this little beauty would have made life much easier on my round-the-world ride.

16. *Cotterless crank removal tool.* Again, make sure it fits your bike. I carry this with me on tour; most people don't.

17. *Universal cotterless crank wrench.* For use with the following item; home tool only, and then only if you work on several cranks of different sizes.

18. *Universal cotterless crankarm puller.* The previous tool removes the "crank-arm fixing bolt" (that wonderful advance of technology beyond the formerly ubiquitous cotter pins); this tool pulls the crankarm to allow access to the bottom bracket hub.

Cotterless crank.
- *A) dust cap*
- *B) fixing bolt*
- *C) washer*
- *D) crankarm*
- *E) chainrings/chainwheels*
- *F) fixed cup*
- *G) bearings*
- *H) spindle*
- *I) adjustable cup*
- *J) front view adjustable cup*
- *K) lockring*

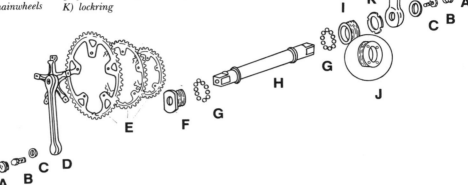

Cotterless crankbolt.

Crankset closeup showing multi-piece crank, cotterless crank dustcap, and smallest of three chainrings.

19. *Universal adjustable cup tool.* This is excellent for home use, but far too heavy for the road. Only on my longest tours do I work on my bottom bracket, and then I use a screwdriver blade tip to adjust the bottom bracket bearing pressure.

20. *Lock ring/fixed cup bottom bracket tool.* For home use only.

21. *Freewheel sprocket tools.* For home use. If you have a large vise you'll need only one; otherwise, two are required to change sprockets. Most people toss their entire freewheels when only a couple of cogs need replacement (the smallest two, usually)—a far less expensive repair than buying all new sprockets plus the center "core" body filled with ball bearings.

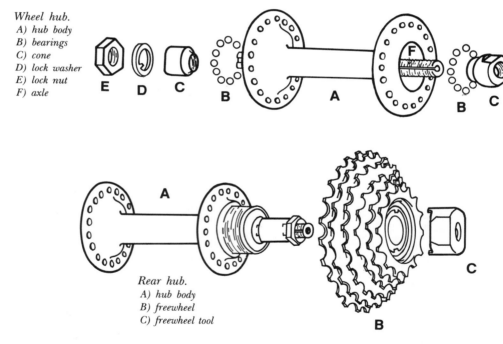

Wheel hub.
A) *hub body*
B) *bearings*
C) *cone*
D) *lock washer*
E) *lock nut*
F) *axle*

Rear hub.
A) *hub body*
B) *freewheel*
C) *freewheel tool*

22. *Sealed bearing tools/roller cam brake tool* (not pictured). Most mountain bikes have "sealed" bearings in one or more areas—pedals, headset, hubs, bottom bracket. Many of these seals can be removed easily with one or more of the tools above, but some are more conveniently removed with specific tools for this purpose. Your dealer will point out these seals to you (and the purpose of the roller cam brake tool) and will either have the appropriate tool for sale or can

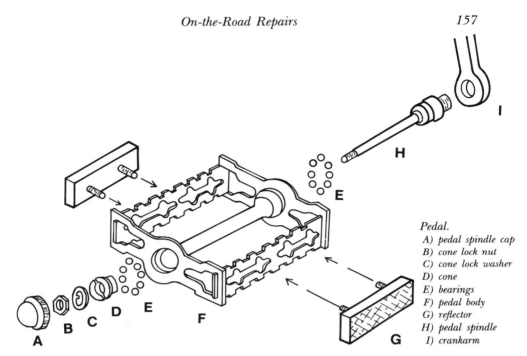

Pedal.
A) *pedal spindle cap*
B) *cone lock nut*
C) *cone lock washer*
D) *cone*
E) *bearings*
F) *pedal body*
G) *reflector*
H) *pedal spindle*
I) *crankarm*

order it. Don't be afraid to ask that he show you how to use these, but be prepared to return to the shop at some time convenient to *him* for the instruction. (If your schedule allows it, try to hit bike shops at times other than Friday afternoons and Saturdays.)

Beyond the tools listed above, tune-up stands of many kinds are available, plus wheel-truing stands, which make that job far easier. Finally, a floor pump with built-in gauge is a must if you ride daily.

SADDLE

A good bike shop will help you determine general saddle position when sizing you for your bike, but most riders find slight adjustments of height, tilt, and position toward or away from the handlebars necessary to produce that perfect fit of cycle and cyclist. Consider yourself very fortunate if your seat post allows these adjustments with only an allen wrench (an allen bolt in the frame—or a lever on a mountain bike—for height adjustments, and a single or double allen fitting beneath the saddle for tilt and forward/backward alterations), or even the more difficult and not very common style that sports two bolts pointing downward from beneath the saddle (which must be reached with a special wrench that is bent like a flattened S). Either of these styles is far easier to work

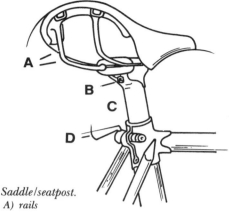

Saddle/seatpost.
A) *rails*
B) *allen head adjustment*
   bolt
C) *seatpost*
D) *quick-release lever*

Seat post bolt (for raising and lowering saddle).

with than the formerly ubiquitous bolt-and-clamp arrangements, which require at least a third hand and a lot of patience.

Chances are, after a couple of weeks of riding you will have the saddle and seatpost where you want them (except, again, with a mountain bike's constant changing of height for safe descents and powerful climbs), and thus won't have to readjust. However, the single allen fitting is a style you might consider not only for ease, but to save weight on a long tour.

Height. Older bikes will require a six-inch crescent on one side of the bolt (running through the frame where the seatpost enters), the channel locks on the other. Holding fast to the bolt head with the channel locks, back off the nut

Under-the-saddle allen head adjustment bolt (for changing tilt and fore/aft position of saddle).

counterclockwise. (By using the crescent on this nut you will avoid chewing up the edges. Be sure to adjust the jaws of this crescent snugly against the nut, so as not to round off these edges.) Then just raise or lower the saddle as desired, and tighten again.

More recent touring bikes will have a round bolt head with small metal tip (designed to fit into a frame slot and thus to hold the bolt steady when moving the nut on the opposite side) or two allen fittings—an even better arrangement for seatpost bolt adjustments. Again, simply loosen the "nutted" side by moving it counterclockwise, raise or lower the seatpost, and tighten. (That part of the post remaining in the frame should be greased lightly, to combat the slight amount of rain that can percolate along it and into the frame, causing rust.)

Tilt. Saddle tilt is a very individual preference. I suggest you begin with no slant whatsoever, and work from there. If your saddle is of the old-style attachment (double clamps with a single metal bar threaded on both ends), use the channel locks (or vise grips if at home) to hold one side fast, and the six-inch crescent to loosen the other side slightly. This will allow the saddle nose to be jockeyed up or down a "notch" at a time (the clamps have notched faces that embrace one another when tight).

With the later saddle attachments you need merely loosen the beneath-the-saddle nuts or underside allen fittings, position the saddle as desired, and tighten.

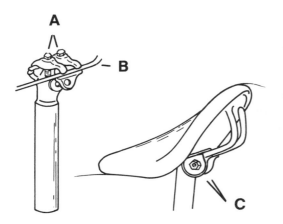

Saddle/seatpost #2

A) *adjustment bolts*
B) *rail*
C) *old-style clamp and bolt*

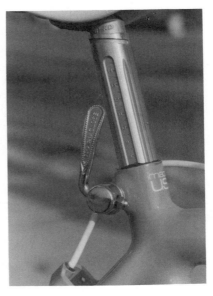

Quick-release seat post lever; notice graduated seat post.

Forward/backward movement. You will recall I mentioned this in the earlier discussion of bike fit. The saddle has the ability to move toward or away from the handlebars along its "rails" (look beneath the saddle for these). This distance, plus top tube and handlebar stem length, allows an extremely personal fit. Pay attention to slight arm, neck, and lower back strain if you are too far from or too close to the bars, and adjust accordingly. Remember that a good bike shop will provide a general fit, but that you must tailor it precisely to your body and riding style. With all style saddles, loosen the attachment of saddle to seatpost (as described above), slide the saddle along its rails, and tighten again.

Side-to-side movement. The saddle nose should of course point directly over the top tube. If it has worked itself off-center, loosen the seatpost bolt in the frame, position correctly, then tighten again.

HANDLEBAR/HEADSET

Don't be scared by all the parts of a headset, for chances are excellent that, as with most things on your bike, you will never have to deal with them on tour. Most riders *never* adjust their headsets, except when erroneously thinking it necessary to raise or lower the bars (handlebars). The following words are provided, therefore, to help you understand this usually neglected portion of your bike, and to facilitate adjustments and repairs if necessary.

First, the headset's job is not to hold the handlebar in place. (This is done by the bar's own expander bolt/wedge assembly, as you'll soon see.) Its purpose, instead, is to secure the fork to the frame in such a manner as to allow free rotation to the right and left. Now look closely at the drawing and you will see how this is performed. The top of the fork is threaded and is held in place in the head tube by the top threaded race (bearing cup). This race, and the fork crown race, are positioned with the top and bottom bearings to allow for rotation. In all my riding the greatest difficulty I've had with headsets (a slight difficulty in turning the bars side to side) was remedied in the following fifteen-minute repair:

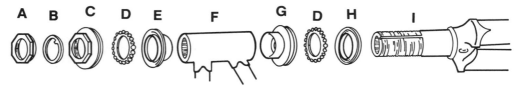

Headset.
A) *locknut*
B) *lock washer*
C) *adjusting cup/top threaded race*
D) *bearings*

E) *top head/set race*
F) *head tube*
G) *bottom head/set race*
H) *fork crown race*
I) *fork*

Handlebar binder bolt (for revolving bars up or down, thereby moving brake hoods closer to the rider); notice stem shifters.

First, using my large crescent when at home, (try the channel locks on the road), I loosened the large locknut at the top of the headset. Next, I loosened the top threaded race, but only slightly, until I could see the bearings inside but *before* they could escape (something that won't happen if you have the ball retainer rings common to many bikes today). I then squirted cycle oil into the mass of bearings, very carefully allowed the fork to slip down a fraction of an inch to expose the bottom bearings, and added oil there. This done, I tightened the top threaded race, then the locknut on top, until there was no upward or downward movement within the headset, but free movement of the fork from side to side.

Bar height adjustment. Notice the expander bolt in the drawing. At the other end of this bolt, inside the head tube, is either an angled expander nut or a wedge nut (an "exterior" or "interior" wedge). When the expander bolt is tightened the angled nut presses against the head tube wall; the wedge-nut type works by drawing the nut up inside the stem, forcing the stem walls out against the head tube.

That's the theory. Now take the second important step in all mechanical repairs: a *close* look at everything that might be affected or at all involved. In the case of lowering or raising bars, many brake assemblies are involved (through the lengthening or shortening of the brake cable). If this is so with your bars, simply disengage the brake cable until the bar is adjusted, then readjust cable length.

Loosen the expander bolt. Don't be concerned if the wedge nut comes off the expander bolt, for it can't fall far. Just turn the bike upside down and the nut will come free. If your bike is brand new your bars can be moved when the expander bolt is loosened, but if not you'll have to rethread the expander bolt several turns into the frozen angled or wedge nut inside the head tube, and

Expander bolt (for raising and lowering bars).

then rap it lightly with a mallet (or something similar). Position the bars as desired—be *sure* to leave at least two full inches of stem inside the head tube—and tighten the expander bolt.

Bars off-center. Sometimes a fall will cause one's bars not to point straight over the wheel. In this case, simply loosen the expander bolt assembly (as above), reposition, and tighten securely.

Loose brake lever. On a mountain bike the allen head fitting is easy to see; reposition and tighten. (In fact, one of the great things about working on an ATB is the obvious nature of most components. The larger size of these

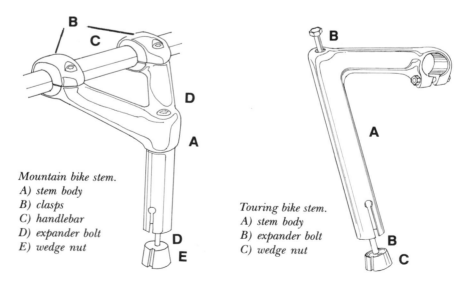

Mountain bike stem.
A) stem body
B) clasps
C) handlebar
D) expander bolt
E) wedge nut

Touring bike stem.
A) stem body
B) expander bolt
C) wedge nut

assemblies also makes us less afraid we'll break something.) It is only slightly more difficult to tighten brake levers on touring bikes.

Disengage or lengthen the brake cable (a quick study of your brake assembly will make evident the ease of this procedure; many have quick-release mechanisms), then depress the brake lever. You will find behind it a slotted bolt head (the old type, to be tightened with a screwdriver), or, more usually, an extremely convenient allen head bolt. Reposition, then tighten.

BRAKES

A thorough study of these assemblies will go far in reducing any fears in working on them. With both touring and mountain bikes you will find a cable leading from the hand brake, through a cable adjustment system of some kind, to the wheel brake component. When the hand brake is squeezed the cable length is shortened, pulling the brake pads toward the wheel rim until contact is made.

Difficulties are encountered when, after much use, the brake pads have worn down, or the cable has stretched or become slightly rusted inside its housing or broken. These two problems are remedied with no tools at all, and can in fact be accomplished from the saddle.

Worn pads and cable stretch. Look back to your cable adjustment assembly, where an "adjustment barrel" of one shape or another shortens the cable when turned counterclockwise. A locknut or lockring beneath the barrel must be loosened to allow adjustment, then tightened again to hold the barrel in place.

After many miles a cable might require more adjustment than that possible through these assemblies. In this case, begin by screwing down the barrel completely (to allow for greater adjustments later), then loosening the "cable anchor bolt" (it will be obvious which bolt-and-nut combination hold the cable in place, as the cable passes directly through it.) Ideally, this should be done with the brake pads pressed against the rim, so as to estimate proper cable position. A "third-hand tool" may be used for this purpose, or a fellow rider. But far more often I simply trip the brake quick-release mechanism (employed on bikes to allow for the fast removal of tires, as this moves the brake pads away from the rim sufficiently to allow the larger tire profile to pass), loosen the cable anchor bolt, take up a slight amount of slack cable, tighten the cable anchor bolt again and reset the brake. It is seldom perfectly correct the first time around, but it will be very close a second time.

Brake pads, by the way, should be set close enough to the rim to ensure the fast, strong application of brake-pad force against the rim with only the

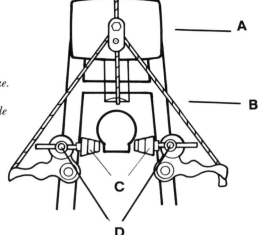

Cantilever brake/sidepull brake.
A) *cable anchor bolt*
B) *center wire/transverse cable*
C) *brake pads*
D) *brake shoe anchor nuts*

slightest movement of the brake handle. With poorly adjusted brakes a precious second is lost while cable slack is taken up through the hard squeezing of the brake handle. Not only can this delay in reaction time be costly, but the pressure of pad against rim will be reduced. Naturally, a well-aligned wheel is necessary if pads are to be mounted close to the rim.

Rubber brake pads once came mounted in their metal "shoes" in such a way that replacement pads were easily installed. The shoes had one end open—that end, of course, that must be mounted *against* the direction of wheel rotation (open end toward the back of the bike). Otherwise the pads would merely shoot forward out of their shoes, leaving you to white-knuckle your way to a thrilling, unassisted stop. Most shoe/pad arrangements today are a single piece, which unfortunately requires a more costly—if idiot-proof—replacement. If you have the older style, just be thoughtful during the replacement.

I mentioned the roller cam brake tool earlier. Its purpose is to hold the brake arms (and thus the pads) in place while working on the cable or arm tension.

Sidepull brake.
A) *adjusting barrel*
B) *lockring*
C) *cable anchor bolt*

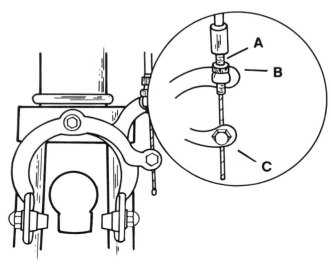

Cable replacement/lubrication. Watch carefully as you remove the broken cable from its housing and you will learn almost all you need to know for replacement. Notice the ball (or pear- or cylinder-shaped) end of the cable, held in place by the brake handle housing. Brake cables come with one end that will fit your particular housing; the other end is to be cut off (carefully, so that the individual metal strands do not fray) to allow its placement into the cable housing, and final entry into the tiny hole in the cable anchor bolt. (I use the side-cutter portion of my needle-nose pliers for this cut when at home, but, as I no longer carry a needle-nose on the road, I have had to resort to more barbaric means. I first crimp the cable strands by placing my screwdriver blade over the cable and tapping the other end with a wrench. Then I work the metal strands back and forth with the channel locks, until they break.)

Once having depressed the brake handle and located the "ball" end of the broken cable, remove the brake cable. Snip off the unnecessary end of the new cable, lightly grease the cable throughout its length, then insert it beneath the brake handle and into the cable housing. Run its cut end through the cable anchor bolt, and adjust pad placement as discussed above. Excess cable can be wound into a ball or cut off.

Sometimes a slight crack in the cable housing, or a drop of water that manages to find its way inside, will cause brakes to "stick." Although the metal brake arms are usually suspected (a drop or two of oil will keep these working well, and can be applied now to determine if these arms or the cable is at fault), it is more likely that rust has formed inside the housing. Simply release the cable at the cable anchor bolt, slip it completely out of its housing, grease, and reattach. (This will be much easier if the free, cut end of the cable has been kept from fraying by a tiny metal "cable clamp"—a soft metal cup that is slipped over the cable end and secured by a squeeze with the channel locks or needle-nose pliers.)

TIRES, SPOKES, AND WHEEL ALIGNMENT

The wheel consists of many parts: hub assembly, spokes, freewheel in the rear, rim, tape (a cloth, plastic, or rubber strip covering the spoke heads, thus protecting the tube from the spokes), tube, tire, and sometimes tire liner (which I suggest for commuting and cactus-area riding). On-the-road repairs required of these parts are usually caused by flat tires and wheels out of alignment. Spoke breakage is extremely infrequent, but will be covered simply to put the mind at ease.

Flats. When the cursing is over, assemble the necessary tools: two tire levers, a six-inch crescent (if your wheels aren't quick-release), tube repair kit or spare tube, and air pump.

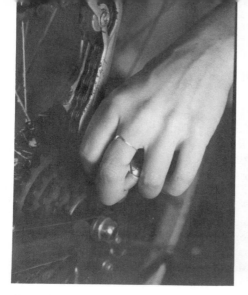 

Preparing to lift back the derailleur housing to allow rear wheel removal. (Most flats appear on the rear wheel.)

"Back" position of rear derailleur, to allow rear wheel removal.

Remove the wheel. To do so you'll have to put your bike on its back, loosen both axle nuts or trip the quick-release lever, and disengage the brake cable—to increase the distance between the brake pads sufficiently for the tire to pass between them. If it's the front wheel, you can simply lift the wheel out of its dropouts at this point. On the rear wheel, shift the chain into the smallest freewheel sprocket, grab the derailleur body and pull it toward the rear of the bike, and lift the wheel free.

Remove the tire and tube from the rim. This is accomplished with the aid of your tire levers (or spoons). Take the lesser angled end of one spoon and, beveled end up, work it underneath the tire bead about a half-inch. (Begin working with the first lever at a point on the wheel opposite the valve stem.) Now push down (toward the spokes) on the tire lever in your hand. Hook the slotted side onto a spoke to hold the tire in place (notice drawing). This frees both hands for the rest of the work.

Take a second lever and, once more, work the tip underneath the tire bead, about an inch from the first lever. Again, push down on your lever, to pop the bead away from its seat in the rim. If you can't do this, move your lever half an inch closer to the first lever. Now continue to work the bead away from the rim all around the wheel, until you have one complete side of the tire free. Then, using your spoon from the opposite side of the wheel, work the second bead off the rim. (You are now working the bead off the rim *away* from you in direction, as of course both beads must come off the same side to free the tire.) Taking one side of the tire off at a time is much easier than trying to force both beads off at once. (Expect a new tire to be more difficult to remove than an old one.)

Tire removal.
A) tire spoon/lever
B) rim
C) tire

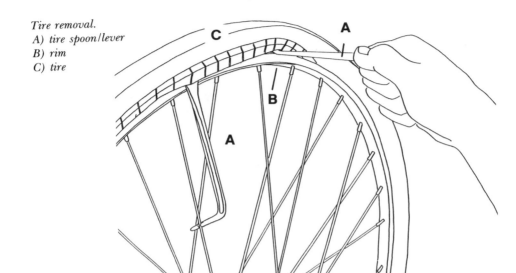

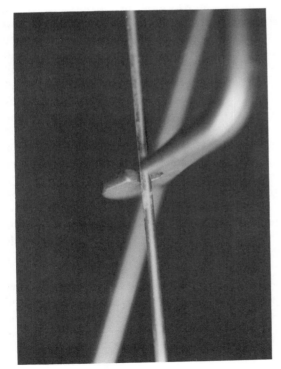

Closeup of indentation in tire iron; avoid buying tire irons without such indentations.

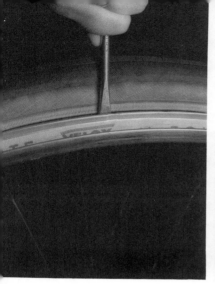 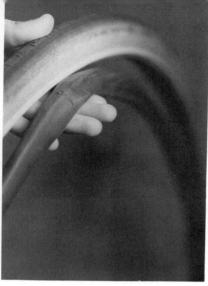 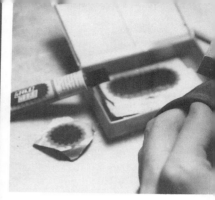

Patch kit showing tube of cement, two patch sizes, tube "rougher" (in hand).

Removal of second bead from tire, freeing tire completely; notice rim tape covering spoke nipple heads.

Tube exposed.

Remove the tube from the tire, checking both the outside and inside of the tire for embedded glass, thorns, and the like. When you're sure that it's clean, move on to the tube. I've had only two holes in my life that leaked so little that I was forced to hold them under water to look for air bubbles. All the other times I merely pumped up the tube and listened for escaping air. (If your tube has a Schrader valve, be sure the air is not escaping from the threaded center valve core. If this core is not screwed tightly into these threads an air leak will result. The proper tool to tighten a valve core is the "valve cover tool," a tiny slotted metal cap that you should buy to replace the worthless black plastic caps present on all tubes sold. If you have a very slow leak, check that your valve core is tight before you remove the wheel from the frame. I've had this problem only once in twenty years, but it's still worth checking.)

When the hole is located, rough up the area with the patch kit scraper. Be sure to do a good job of it, short of putting additional holes in the tube, and be sure to roughen an area a bit larger than the size of the patch.

Apply the glue, a bit more than necessary to cover the patch area. Most kits suggest waiting until the glue is dry to apply the patch. Heed their advice. Hurry this step and there's a good chance you'll be taking the wheel off the bike again a few miles down the road. Be careful not to touch the patch side that goes on the tube, and when it is in place press the edges of the patch with a tire spoon.

When the patch appears to be holding well along the edges, pump a very slight amount of air into the tube to avoid its getting wrinkles when it is placed back inside the tire. Put the tube in the tire, push the valve stem through the valve stem hole in the rim, and reseat one of the beads. Once one side of the tire—one bead—is in place, begin reseating the second bead. (Removing all air at this point reduces the chance of puncture.) In taking off a tire one begins *opposite* the stem; in replacing it one begins work *at* the stem and works away from it in both directions, being sure to keep the stem pointing straight up. Riders who fail to do this, or who ride with low air pressure in their tires (which causes the tube to shift and the valve stem to angle out of the hole), cause wearing of the stem along its side and base. Once a hole occurs in the valve stem the entire tube is shot, for stems can't hold a patch.

You will probably be able to reseat all except about six inches of the beads without tools. At this point, use your tire spoon in the opposite manner than before—beveled end down.

If both beads are properly seated, and the stem is still perpendicular, inflate the tire to its desired pressure. Do this before you put the wheel back on the bike, for it will mean less to mess with if you've goofed with the patch. But don't worry. A chimp can master a patch kit.

If the tire remains hard for a minute replace the wheel, tighten axle nuts or the quick-release, reengage the chain if it is the rear wheel, *and* reset your brakes.

Freewheel removal. This is an unfortunate necessity if a rear wheel spoke breaks on the freewheel side (which is almost the *only* place they break, due to the "dishing" discussed in an earlier chapter); but today's "pocket vises" make this repair possible on the road.

Remove the rear wheel, and unscrew and remove the quick-release mechanism. Slide the thin shaft of the quick-release through the pocket vise, freewheel tool (pictured), and freewheel. Center the two prongs of the pocket vise over the handlebar stem, engage the flat sides of the freewheel tool (with the wheel above it), take hold of the wheel at the three and nine o'clock positions and turn counterclockwise. If you're a strong rider, and if the freewheel has not been off the wheel before, you'll have to work at getting it off. Once removed, the spoke heads are visible and replacement can begin.

Freewheel removal tool.

Separating freewheel from rear wheel (where most broken spokes appear).

During those long years before the pocket vise was invented, I struggled with other methods of "breaking" the freewheel. The easiest is finding a regular vise at a home or garage, for the freewheel tool then is set into the vise jaws with its splined or notched teeth pointing up, and the wheel is simply fit over it and turned free. A second relatively easy method is to locate a huge crescent or pipe wrench, place the tire standing up in front of you with freewheel on the right side, engage the freewheel tool into both the freewheel and wrench, and press *downward*.

The hardest of all removals is with the seven-inch channel locks taking the place of a larger wrench, and a shock cord wrapped around its handles to hold it together and provide the hand some sort of protection. I've done this only once, when there was no alternative, and it took its toll on both my tool and me. Buy a pocket vise.

But what if you haven't a quick-release wheel? I've solved that problem (for use with my mountain bike wheels and their large axles) by drilling out the tiny hole in the pocket vise sufficiently to accept the axle, and then balancing the wheel and freewheel tool in place over the pocket vise. It's a bit less stable, but it works.

Removing spoke protector plate.

Spoke replacement/wheel alignment. Let's begin with an analysis of the thin, spindly spoke. If you've never thought of it, ponder for a moment how such slender pillars of metal can hold up the weight of a bike, rider, and his gear, while being light enough to spin almost effortlessly in circles around a hub. Now look closely at it; a long shank, threads at the top where it screws into the nipple (protruding through the rim hole and holding the spoke in place and under desired tension), and at the other end a right-angle crook that holds it in the hub. That sharp, right-angle bend is the danger point, the place where, when stress becomes too great, life ends. It is curtains for the spoke, curses for the rider, and an opportunity for the spoke wrench to see daylight once again.

More common, however, is a spoke that simply needs adjustment to help realign (make "true" again) a wheel. Wheels can be out of true in two ways: they can sway from side to side, and they can have high and low spots, which is referred to as being "out of round." Look closely at your wheel. Notice that the spokes reach out to the rim from both sides of the hub. Focus upon one spoke and think what tightening (shortening the length of) that single spoke will do. The rim will be pulled in two directions at the same time when the spoke is tightened, or moved back in two directions if loosened. Tighten the spoke and

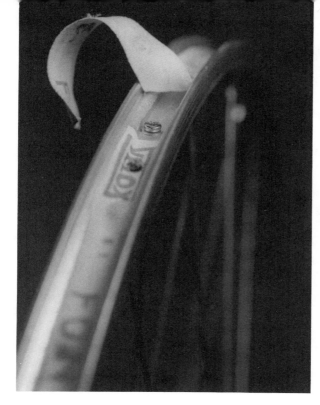

Rim tape removed, slotted (for screwdriver) spoke nipple shown.

the rim will be (1) pulled closer to the hub, and (2) pulled in the direction of the side of the hub to which the other end of the spoke is attached. Loosen the spoke and the opposite movement will occur. Tighten a spoke coming from the other side of the hub and the rim will move in that direction.

"Truing" a wheel is most quickly and successfully accomplished with the assistance of a truing stand, and with the wheel off the bike, the tire, tube, and rim tape removed. The stands have small moveable metal indicators that one slides ever closer to the rim from both sides as the spoke adjustments bring the wheel increasingly into alignment. This can also be done without a stand, using the bike itself to hold the wheel and one's thumb in place of the metal slides. In fact, since spokes break while riding, and because wheels become untrue generally while I'm touring, I've almost always done this repair while far away from home.

Let us imagine you have broken a spoke on the rear wheel. Begin the repair by flipping your bike on its back, and removing the wheel, tire, tube, and rim tape. If the break is on the freewheel side, remove the freewheel. Put the wheel back on the bike without tightening axle nuts or quick-release. (The spoke can be replaced with the wheel off the bike, but I find it much easier to work with the wheel when it is back in place.)

Remove the broken spoke. This is very easy, for spokes break at the bevel, and can then be taken out by pulling from the nipple end.

Take the nipple from the new spoke. Look at the rear hub, and concentrate on the spokes closest to the one that broke. If you see two spoke heads next to the empty hole in the hub you know that your new spoke must enter from the other side, to follow the alternating pattern around the entire hub. Guide the spoke into the hole. (Don't be afraid to bend the spoke a bit.) Once it is completely through, look at the next closest spoke that enters the hub in the same direction as your replacement spoke. This will be your guide on lacing your replacement—how many spokes you must cross, and which to go over or under with the new spoke. (You'll have to bend the spoke even more here; be sure to bend it along its entire length, thereby not putting a crimp in it.)

Put the nipple into the rim, and thread the new spoke into it. Tighten the spoke until it has approximately the same tension as the rest, and then align the wheel (following the procedure below).

I prefer to align wheels with tire, tube, and rim tape removed. This allows for more accurate truing and exposes the screw head of the spoke nipple for adjustment with a screwdriver (necessary if you've rounded the nipple with the spoke wrench). It also allows you to *see* if too much spoke extends through the nipple head, in which case the metal file blade of the Swiss army knife can be used to shorten it. (If you've purchased spare spokes of the proper length you won't be troubled by protrusion.) Restore your freewheel to its proper location, and replace your wheel in the frame (if it isn't already there) as it will be when

Closeup rear wheel spoking pattern.

Closeup front wheel spoking pattern.

you ride. Tighten axle nuts or close the quick-release lever, but keep the brakes free.

Standing behind your wheel, with the bike still on its back, spin the wheel with your hand and note the "wobble"—movement from side to side.

Determine the extent of the wobble by placing your thumb next to the wheel rim (with the palm of your hand resting on the chainstay), so that your thumbnail lightly touches the rim at every point except for the wobble. At that point the rim will reach out and smack your thumbnail; your job is to pull that wobble back into line with the rest of the rim.

Check the tension of the spokes in the area of the wobble. Chances are, they will be a bit looser than the rest of the spokes in the wheel. Tighten the spoke at the center of the wobble—just a bit at a time, watching its effect upon the rim—then move on to the spokes on either side. (Read the next two paragraphs before proceeding.)

But how much do you tighten a spoke? And what if two spokes appear to sit right smack in the middle of the problem area? Easy. Just recall that spokes reach out to the rim from both sides of the hub. Naturally, tightening a spoke coming from the right side pulls the rim toward the right; from the left hub side, to the left. If your wobble is to the right, you'll be tightening the spokes that come from the left side of your hub. I always start off with a slight adjustment—about a half-turn for the spoke at wobble center, one-quarter turn for spokes on either side, one-eighth turn for the next two spokes.

On occasion you might have to loosen some spokes and tighten others in the wobble area to produce a true wheel, especially if you have trued your wheel several times before. In loosening spokes, follow the same pattern as above; more toward wobble center, less thereafter.

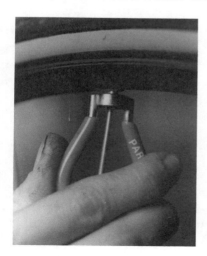

Attachment of new spoke to nipple end after replacement.

When your thumbnail-guide tells you all is well, you have two final things to do. First, check your spokes for approximately the same tension on all. You won't be perfect on this, but at least try to be close or you'll be aligning your wheel again real soon. Second, step to the side of your bike, spin the wheel and check for its "round." If you have one high spot, tighten the spokes slightly in this area—to pull the rim toward the hub a bit. But be sure to watch that you don't lose your side-to-side true as you do this.

Let me add that I find wheel alignment to be the most delicate, and thus the most difficult, repair on a bike. Go easy at first, and try to be patient. Your spokes will appreciate it.

WHEEL BEARINGS

Most touring cyclists are seldom out so long as to require wheel bearing service, and thus do not have to carry cone wrenches. ("Cones" are the threaded, cone-shaped pieces named for the tapering end that rests against the bearings; the other end is squared off to fit the wrench used to adjust pressure against the bearings.) Many of these mechanisms are today "sealed," thus requiring no maintenance, and under normal conditions one needn't give one's cones a thought on tour. However, I pack the thin cone wrenches so that I can make the proper adjustments should anything go wrong on my longer rides, and, of course, when I pull full-bearing maintenance during winter cross-country tours.

Should you decide to readjust your cone-bearing pressure, hold the lock-nut on one side of the hub (see drawing) with a crescent wrench or channel locks, and use a second wrench to loosen the locknut on the opposite hub side. Unscrew the locknut completely, putting it somewhere so that you'll not kick it as you continue working. Next, remove the keyed lock washer ("keyed" refers to the small pointed flange of metal on the inside of the washer, which fits the groove on the axle). Now you can hold the locknut on the opposite hub side immobile, while very carefully adjusting cone pressure against the bearings on the dismantled side. As with so many adjustments on a bike, you are looking for that perfect point that allows free rotation of the wheel, but no lateral wheel sway.

DERAILLEURS

Derailler in French means "to take from the rails"; in cycling it refers to the movement of one's chain from one sprocket to another. This is accomplished through a series of shifters, gear cables, and front and rear derailleurs.

Basically, a gear cable runs from the shifter (also called shift lever, shift handle, or gear handle), along the down tube and chainstay, through a cable-adjusting barrel (similar in principle to that found on brakes), to a cable clamp bolt on the changer (another name for derailleur). When you pull back on the shift lever (or push forward on a mountain bike's thumb shifter) you tighten the cable, which causes the derailleur to lift the chain from a smaller sprocket, and set it upon a larger one. Naturally, there are limits to how far in either direction you would wish your chain to go; this limitation is established by "high" and "low" gear-adjusting screws. The high gear screw on rear derailleurs keeps the chain from moving beyond the smallest sprocket and falling off the freewheel; the low gear screw keeps the chain from moving beyond the largest sprocket and attacking your spokes. The third screw present on some changers is an "angle" screw. Chains, like cables, stretch over time, thereby changing the angle of the derailleur and thus its performance. This angle screw allows for taking up this tiny bit of slack by resetting the proper angle in relation to the freewheel.

Below the derailleur housing are two pulleys, or rollers. Notice that the chain rolls over one and under the second. The top pulley is the "jockey" or "guide" pulley—named for its job of jockeying the chain into place over a sprocket. The bottom one is the "tension" pulley, for it takes up the slack in the chain when the derailleur moves from a larger to a smaller sprocket. The final thing you should notice are the points of lubrication—small holes in the derailleur body that run toward the internal springs. Apply a couple of drops of oil each month, and wipe off the excess.

Derailleur adjustment. Once again it is necessary to remind ourselves that everything on a bike is mechanical and understandable, not magic. For some reason riders appear to dread touching their derailleurs, and thus needlessly put up with inexact gear changes, dropped chains, and an inability to shift into particular gears.

By far the most frequent "transmission" problem encountered by cyclists can be solved with a few slight turns of the "high" and "low" gear-adjusting screws. Let's say your chain cannot quite make it up onto the largest sprocket of the freewheel. Recalling that the larger freewheel sprockets provide the lower (easier to pedal) gears, simply give the "L" screw of the rear derailleur a quarter- or half-turn counterclockwise to start. If your chain falls off the smallest sprocket (highest gear) of your freewheel, turn the "H" screw on the rear derailleur clockwise, thereby limiting the chain's movement away from the freewheel.

Similar problems with the chainrings in front can be solved through the adjustment of the front derailleur limiting screws. Look closely inside the derailleur housing and you'll be able actually to see these limiting screws making contact with the body.

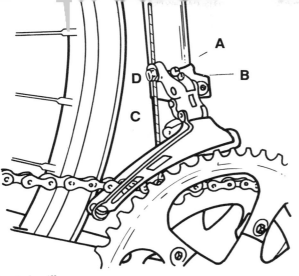

Front derailleur.
A) low gear adjusting screw
B) high gear adjusting screw
C) cage
D) cable anchor bolt

Front derailleur set screws.

Let us go back to the problem of the chain's not quite reaching up onto the largest freewheel sprocket. You have adjusted the "L" screw, can in fact see that the housing is not making contact with this limiting screw, and yet the chain cannot quite fall into place. In such a case (very infrequent) the problem is not with the derailleur, but with the cable. It has stretched over time, and now must be readjusted. Most recent bikes have gear cable adjustment barrels

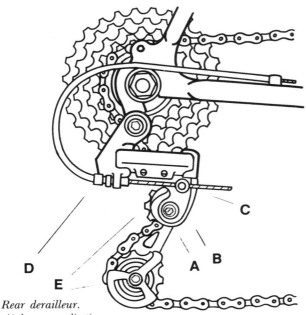

Rear derailleur.
A) low gear adjusting screw
B) high gear adjusting screw
C) cable anchor bolt
D) adjusting barrel
E) pulleys

Set screws for rear derailleur
(notice "L" and "H" for low
and high).

to remove this slack quickly and easily (as with the brake cable adjustment systems); if yours does not have such, you must loosen the "cable fixing bolt" (which clamps the cable into place on the derailleur housing), shorten the cable slightly, and then tighten the fixing bolt again.

Cable replacement. Today's cables break very infrequently, but you must know how to replace one if it happens while you're on tour. Otherwise, if it is the rear cable (as it almost always is because of its far more frequent use), you'll have to pedal all the way home in your hardest gear.

Begin by loosening the cable fixing bolt of whichever derailleur is affected by the broken cable. Remove the cable. (If the rear derailleur is involved, screw the cable adjusting barrel clockwise, into the derailleur body, until it stops.) Next, move to the other end of the cable and begin the very careful dismantling of your gear shift lever assembly. I always lay out the pieces in the same sequence as they are removed, so that I won't be wracked by indecision over which piece comes next when I'm rebuilding it. Remove the lever-fixing bolt (most recent models have a bale device on top) and cover, install a new cable (cutting off the unnecessary end, as you did with the brake cable), then replace the cover and fixing bolt. Place the lever in its most relaxed (no tension being applied to the cable) position. Feed the new cable through the cable housing (I grease mine slightly before doing this), then through the cable adjusting barrel (on rear derailleurs), and onto the cable fixing bolt.

When replacing a rear derailleur cable, place the chain on the smallest front chainring. Pull the cable slightly taut (not so much that the derailleur body moves) and secure it by tightening the cable fixing bolt. The rear derailleur pulleys should be in line with the smallest freewheel sprocket at this point. If they are not, turn the high gear adjusting screw until that alignment is attained; if it cannot be reached with the adjusting screw it means you have pulled the cable too tight. Loosen the cable fixing bolt and readjust the cable tension.

To make the low gear adjustment, carefully shift the chain onto the largest freewheel sprocket; if this can't be done, turn the low gear adjusting screw counterclockwise until it can. Then adjust the thumb shifter until the rear derailleur pulleys are in perfect line with the largest freewheel sprocket, and turn the low gear adjusting screw clockwise—into the changer body—until you feel resistance.

When replacing a front derailleur cable, place the chain on the largest rear and smallest front sprockets. Then turn the low gear adjusting screw until there's a slight clearance between the chain and the inside plate of the chain cage (chain guide). If this cannot be done it means you have pulled the cable too taut; loosen the cable anchor bolt, correct the tension, and retighten.

Next, place the chain on the smallest rear and largest front sprockets.

Then turn the high gear adjusting screw until there is a slight clearance between the chain and the outside plate of the chain cage. When these adjustments to the rear and front derailleurs have been made, switch the chain through all possible gear combinations. In each gear you should be able to position the derailleurs so that the chain does not make noise and does not rub against the metal inner and outer plates.

CHAIN

Beyond the occasional drop of oil after much wet weather, the tourer need not worry too much about his chain. I've never had to clean one thoroughly on tour, and if starting out with a good one (worn out chains have considerable lateral sway, are noisy even when lubricated, and should be replaced before a tour) I never encountered problems requiring disassembly. However, I have had two very infrequent problems: frozen and broken links.

You will need a chain rivet tool to free frozen links, and to add a new link if one breaks. Look at this tool very carefully while going through the following instructions.

Frozen and broken links. When a link becomes frozen (a condition often caused by insufficient lubrication) it makes itself known by jumping over the teeth in the sprockets, or by causing the rear derailleur to jerk forward suddenly as it passes over the jockey and tension pulleys. Elevate your rear wheel and turn the crank to find the culprit link, and, when you find it, coat it with a light oil and work the link with your fingers. This may free it. If not, you'll have to employ the tool.

When viewed from the side, the chain tool looks like a wide "U," with two shorter "walls" of metal between. Place the tool in front of you with the handle to the right side. Twist the handle counterclockwise to remove the rivet "pin" from view. Now, take the chain and place it over the first of these inner walls from the right side. (It will usually be somewhat wider than the left-hand wall.) Notice, when you view your chain tool from the top, that these walls have an open space in the middle, and the chain roller rests in it with the "plates" on either side of the wall. (Look at an individual link. Each is made up of these metal side plates, small bars called "rollers" to engage the teeth of sprockets, and tiny rivets to hold the side plates and rollers together.)

To free a frozen link, place it as described above on the right-hand wall of the chain rivet tool. Turn the tool handle clockwise until the tool rivet pin touches the chain rivet. As you turn the handle more, notice how the plates move slightly farther apart. Most often only the slightest rivet adjustment is necessary to free the link. Be sure not to push the chain rivet flush with the side plate, for its length is such that it should extend slightly past the plates on both sides. If it is necessary to push the rivet flush to free the link, simply turn the chain over in the tool and apply pressure against the opposite end of the rivet.

In the case of a chain break, you must remove the broken link completely and replace it with a spare. This requires that the chain rivet be driven out of one side plate past the roller, yet still remaining in place in the far side plate. (I *know* this sounds very confusing. But it won't be when you're attempting the repair.) Keeping the rivet in the far side plate can be a little tricky at first, so I suggest you run through this procedure a couple of times before a very long ride. Bike shops will often have lengths of old chains with which you can practice.

Place the chain over the left-hand wall of your chain tool, and turn the handle clockwise until the tool rivet pin touches the chain rivet. Then continue turning very carefully, until the roller can be pulled free, but with the chain rivet still in the far side plate. Install the new link by turning the chain tool around and driving the chain rivet through the new roller and side plate. You'll probably find that it is frozen when replaced. If so, simply place this link on the right-hand plate and free it, following the directions above.

Lubrication and cleaning. On touring bikes I prefer a single drop of oil on each roller, followed by a rubbing of the entire chain with a lightly oiled cloth. I then turn the cranks a few times and wait several minutes for the lubricant to penetrate past the rivets. Next, I wipe the chain with a dry cloth, for visible oil does nothing to minimize friction and merely attracts dust. For mountain-bike riding on dirt roads and trails I choose a "dri-lube" or other nonpetroleum synthetic lubricant.

For a quick cleaning while at home I use the Vetta Chain Cleaner, a plastic brush-and-solvent reservoir that mounts on the chain while it is in place on the bike. Should you have a muddy encounter on tour, however, you'll have no choice but to remove the chain, swish it about in a coffee can of kerosene or similar cleaner, and donate a toothbrush to the effort for particularly gummed-up areas.

After many thousands of miles you will have to replace your old chain. At this time it may be necessary to replace the smallest two cogs of your freewheel, for these wear down more quickly than the other cogs, and thus are formed to the stretched-out links of your old chain.

A final suggestion: learn about your bike before your tour and you won't waste time fearing breakdowns. Bicycles are amazingly rugged and will stand a terrific amount of abuse. But they perform best when their riders know them well enough to sense a tiny problem before it can grow.

POSTSCRIPT

THIS WILL BE brief. In fact, I add these few sentences for two simple reasons: first, I hate ending books on a cold, mechanical note; second, after so many pages of in-depth analysis of the physical side of cycling I feel a need to emphasize what I think counts most in this sport—one's mental attitude. As I stated in the Introduction, the key to happy, satisfying cycle touring lies less in performance than in a perception of the activity as travel on two wheels.

Let this thought guide you as you research your route, plan your daily distances, determine what will make you feel you've had a "successful" tour. I have already said I try, as much as possible, to allow the places and people met along the way to determine each day's progress. This may not work for you, but some degree of it (hoping to average sixty miles rather than eighty, or thirty-five instead of fifty) in your planning will help to remove from your ride the pressure of mileage. It is, after all, *your* tour. Riding with someone else's notion of progress isn't any fun.

Finally, if you would like to begin touring but hesitate to start off by yourself, I suggest an excellent half step toward your first self-contained tour—the supported, organized rides offered by a host of companies nationwide. In the last year I have ridden with four very different companies, and I enjoyed all of them immensely.

With a large *Backroads* group I rode a relatively easy, paved route through the Canadian Rockies, ate lavish meals cooked in camp by the three tour leaders, and met cyclists who spanned five decades in age and all professions. On an

even more recent ride with *Rim Tours* I mountain-biked the desert beauty of the arduous White Rim Trail of Utah's Canyonlands National Park. I had taken the same ride solo six months before, and loved it. This time, however, I didn't have to carry my own gear and thus enjoyed the terrain even more. And having others along to share the experience didn't make it *more* enjoyable, just very enjoyable in a different way than when I rode the route alone.

The third of my group-tour experiences was an ATB ride with a company called *The Road Less Traveled,* which offers "customized tours of the backroads of the Greater Yellowstone Ecosystem." One has options of tours fully supported or self-contained, group or solo (with just the guide), completely planned or "custom-designed" by yourself. It was a wonderful way to view the Yellowstone region, and it gave me a chance to experience the kind of "partner" touring of my younger days.

The most recent of my group rides was with *Backcountry Bicycle Tours,* a mountain-bike company that travels both paved and dirt roads throughout the fantastically scenic Intermountain West, and offers a New Zealand trip as well. I joined them for their "Yellowstone Highcountry Adventure" tour, and though I had ridden most of this area before I must admit I never saw it quite like this. Backcountry's best attribute in my opinion is the homey feeling provided by the guides and owners, Doug and Carmen McSpadden; I can't imagine not touring with them again, or failing to keep in touch. But running a close second in good points is the enormous research these folks put into their trails. "Backcountry" is a perfect name for the approach of quiet roads, bucolic settings, and inns and bed-and-breakfasts that welcomed us as family. (Camping trips are also available.)

One need only look at the back pages of any bike magazine to find the addresses of dozens of tour companies across the nation. (Addresses of the four I've toured with can be found in the Appendix.) As I said, they're a great way to obtain a painless first taste of touring, or, for even longtime solo cyclists, the camaraderie and fun of a group.

My hope from the beginning has been that this book will help you hit the road, and enjoy all aspects of your travels. Train hard, plan wisely, and don't be in a hurry. Years from now you will scarcely recall how many miles you did or didn't do. But the people and places you experience will be with you forever.

And if you're bored some evening in your tent, and have the candlelight to spare, I'd love to hear about your ride:

Dennis Coello
470 South 1300 East, #409
Salt Lake City, Utah 84102.

APPENDIX A: *GEAR CHART FOR 27" WHEEL*

Number of teeth in front sprocket

	24	26	28	30	32	34	36	38	40	42	44	45	46	47	48	49	50	52	53	54	55	56
12	54	58.5	63	67.5	72	76.5	81	85.5	90	94.5	99	101.2	103.5	105.7	108	110.2	112.3	117	119.3	121.5	122.7	126
13	49.8	54	58.1	62.3	66.4	70.6	74.7	78.9	83.1	87	91.4	93.4	95.5	97.6	99.7	101.8	103.9	108	110	112.1	114.2	116.3
14	46.2	50.1	54	57.8	61.7	65.5	69.5	73.3	77.1	81.2	84.9	86.7	88.7	90.6	92.6	94.5	96.4	100.3	102.2	104.1	106	108
15	43.2	46.8	50.4	54	57.6	61.1	64.8	68.4	72	75.6	79.2	81	82.8	84.6	86.4	88.2	90	93.6	95.4	97.2	99	100.8
16	40.5	43.7	47.2	50.6	54	57.2	60.9	64.1	67.5	70.9	74.3	76	77.6	79.3	81	82.7	84.4	87.8	89.4	91.1	92.8	94.5
17	38.1	41.2	44.4	47.6	50.8	54	57.2	60.3	63.5	66.7	69.9	71.5	73.1	74.6	76.2	77.8	79.4	82.6	84.1	85.7	87.3	88.9
18	36	39	42	45	48	51	54	57	60	63	66	67.5	69	70.5	72	73.5	75	78	79.5	81	82.5	84
19	34.1	36.8	39.7	42.6	45.5	48.2	51.1	54	56.8	59.7	62.5	64	65.4	66.8	68.2	69.6	71.1	73.9	75.3	76.7	78.1	79.5
20	32.4	35.1	37.8	40.5	43.2	45.9	48.7	51.3	54	56.7	59.4	60.8	62.1	63.4	64.8	66.2	67.5	70.2	71.5	72.9	74.5	75.6
21	30.8	33.4	36	38.6	41.1	43.7	46.4	48.9	51.4	54	56.6	57.9	59.1	60.4	61.7	63	64.3	66.9	68.1	69.4	70.7	72
22	29.4	31.9	34.3	36.8	39.2	41.6	44.2	46.6	49.1	51.5	54	55.2	56.5	57.6	58.9	60.1	61.4	63.8	65	66.2	67.5	68.7
23	28.1	30.5	32.8	35.2	37.5	39.9	42.4	44.6	47	49.3	51.6	52.8	54	55.2	56.3	57.5	58.7	61	62.2	63.6	64.5	65.7
24	27	29.2	31.5	33.7	36	38.2	40.5	42.8	45	47.3	49.5	50.7	51.8	52.9	54	55.1	56.3	58.6	59.6	60.7	61.8	63
25	25.9	28	30.2	32.4	34.6	36.7	38.9	41	43.2	45.4	47.5	48.6	49.7	50.8	51.8	52.9	54	56.2	57.2	58.3	59.4	60.4
26	24.9	27	29	31.2	33.2	35.3	37.4	39.5	41.5	43.6	45.7	46.7	47.8	48.8	49.9	50.9	51.9	54	55	56	57.1	58.1
28	23.1	25	27	28.9	30.8	32.8	34.7	36.6	38.6	40.5	42.4	43.4	44.4	45.3	46.3	47.2	48.2	50.1	51.1	52	53	54
29	22.4	24.2	26.1	28	29.8	31.6	33.5	35.4	37.2	39	41	41.9	42.8	43.8	44.7	45.6	46.5	48.4	49.4	50.3	51.2	52.1
30	21.6	23.4	25.2	27	28.8	30.6	32.4	34.2	36	37.8	39.6	40.5	41.4	42.3	43.2	44.1	45	46.8	47.7	48.6	49.5	50.4
31	20.9	22.6	24.4	26.2	27.9	29.6	31.4	33.1	34.8	36.6	38.3	39.2	40.1	41	41.8	42.6	43.5	45.2	46.2	47	47.9	48.8
32	20.3	22	23.6	25.3	27	28.7	30.4	32.1	33.7	35.4	37.2	38	38.8	39.7	40.5	41.4	42.2	43.9	44.7	45.5	46.4	47.3
33	19.6	21.3	22.9	24.6	26.2	27.8	29.5	31.1	32.7	34.4	36	36.8	37.6	38.5	39.3	40.1	40.9	42.6	43.4	44.2	45	45.9
34	19.1	20.6	22.2	23.8	25.4	27	28.6	30.2	31.8	33.3	35	35.7	36.5	37.4	38.1	38.9	39.7	41.3	42.1	42.9	43.6	44.5

Number of teeth in rear sprocket

APPENDIX B: *GEAR CHART FOR 26" WHEEL**

Number of teeth in front sprocket

	24	26	28	30	32	34	36	38	40	42	44	46	48	50	52
12	52	56.3	60.7	65	69.3	73.4	78	82.3	86.7	91	95.3	99.7	104	108.3	112.7
13	48	52	56	60	64	68	72	76	80	84	88	92	96	100	104
14	44.6	48.3	52	55.8	59.4	63.1	66.9	70.6	74.3	78	81.7	85.4	89.1	92.9	96.6
15	41.6	45.1	48.5	52	55.5	58.9	62.4	65.9	69.3	72.8	76.3	79.7	83.2	86.7	90.1
16	39	42.3	45.5	48.8	52	55.3	58.5	61.8	65	68.3	71.5	74.8	78	81.3	84.5
17	36.7	39.8	42.8	45.9	48.9	52	55.1	58.1	61.2	64.2	67.3	70.4	73.4	76.5	79.5
18	34.7	37.6	40.4	43.3	46.2	49.1	52	54.9	57.8	60.7	63.6	66.4	69.3	72.2	75.1
19	32.8	35.6	38.3	41.1	43.8	46.5	49.3	52	54.7	57.8	60.2	62.9	65.7	68.4	71.2
20	31.2	33.8	36.4	39	41.6	44.2	46.8	49.4	52	54.6	57.2	59.8	62.4	65	67.6
21	29.7	32.2	34.7	37.1	39.6	42.1	44.6	47	49.5	52	54.5	57	59.4	61.9	63.4
22	28.4	30.7	33.1	35.5	37.8	40.2	42.5	44.9	47.3	49.6	52	54.4	56.7	59.1	61.5
23	27.1	29.4	31.7	33.9	36.2	38.4	40.7	43	45.2	47.5	49.7	52	54.3	56.5	58.8
24	26	28.2	30.3	32.5	34.7	36.8	39	41.2	43.3	45.5	47.7	49.8	52	54.2	56.3
25	25	27	29.1	31.2	33.3	35.4	37.4	39.5	41.6	43.7	45.8	47.8	49.9	52	54.1
26	24	26	28	30	32	34	36	38	40	42	44	46	48	50	52
27	23.1	25	27	28.9	30.8	32.7	34.7	36.6	38.5	40.4	42.4	44.3	46.2	48.1	50.1
28	22.3	24.1	26	27.9	29.7	31.6	33.4	35.3	37.1	39	40.9	42.7	44.6	46.4	48.3
29	21.5	23.3	25.1	26.9	28.7	30.5	32.3	34.1	35.9	37.7	39.4	41.2	43	44.8	46.6
30	20.8	22.5	24.3	26	27.7	29.5	31.2	32.9	34.7	36.4	38.1	39.9	41.6	43.3	45.1
31	20.1	21.8	23.5	25.2	26.8	28.5	30.2	31.9	33.5	35.2	36.9	38.6	40.3	41.9	43.6
32	19.5	21.1	22.8	24.4	26	27.6	29.3	30.9	32.5	34.1	35.8	37.4	39	40.6	42.3
33	18.9	20.5	22.1	23.6	25.2	26.7	28.4	29.9	31.5	33.1	34.7	36.2	37.8	39.4	41
34	18.4	19.9	21.4	22.9	24.5	26	27.5	29.1	30.6	32.1	33.6	35.2	36.7	38.2	39.8
35	17.8	19.3	20.8	22.3	23.8	25.3	26.7	28.2	29.7	31.2	32.7	34.2	35.7	37.1	38.6
36	17.3	18.8	20.2	21.7	23.1	24.6	26	27.4	28.9	30.3	31.8	33.2	34.7	36.1	37.6

(Left vertical axis label: Number of teeth in rear sprocket)

inch gear $= \dfrac{\text{\# teeth in front sprocket}}{\text{\# teeth in rear sprocket}} \times$ wheel diameter in inches

Example: $\dfrac{48}{13} \times 26 = 96$ inch gear

(Compute linear distance traveled with each crank rotation by multiplying "inch gear" by pi = 3.14)

Example: $96 \times 3.14 = 301.44''$ (or $25.12'$ linear distance)

---

*Some people contend that the higher profile tire on 26" mountain-bike wheels makes a separate gear chart unnecessary, as the ultimate difference between a 27" touring tire and the ATB wheel is insignificant. I have measured the difference, computed it for a two-hundred-mile tour, and cannot agree.

APPENDIX C: *Bicycle Organizations*

BICYCLE USA (League of American Wheelmen)
Suite 209
6707 Whitestone Road
Baltimore, MD 21207
(301) 944-3399

AMERICAN YOUTH HOSTELS (AYH)
National Office
P.O. Box 37613
Washington, DC 20013-7613
(202) 783-6161

BIKECENTENNIAL
P.O. Box 8308
Missoula, MT 59807
(406) 721-1776

NATIONAL OFF-ROAD BICYCLE ASSOCIATION (NORBA)
P.O. Box 1901
Chandler, AZ 85244
(602) 961-0635

APPENDIX D: *Bike Magazines*

BICYCLE USA
Suite 209
6707 Whitestone Road
Baltimore, MD 21207 (magazine for members)

BICYCLE GUIDE
711 Boylston Street
Boston, MA 02116

BICYCLING
33 E. Minor Street
Emmaus, PA 18049

CYCLIST
20916 Higgins Court
Torrance, CA 90501

FAT TIRE FLYER
P.O. Box 757
Fairfax, CA 94930

MOUNTAIN BIKE
P.O. Box 989
Crested Butte, CO 81224

MOUNTAIN BIKING
10968 Via Frontera
San Diego, CA 92127

MOUNTAIN BIKE ACTION
P.O. Box 9502
Mission Hills, CA 91345-9502

APPENDIX E: *Pannier Companies*

CANNONDALE
9 Brookside Place
Georgetown, CT 06829

ECLIPSE
P.O. Box 7370
Ann Arbor, MI 48107

KANGAROO BAGGS
3891 North Ventura Avenue
Ventura, CA 93001

KIRTLAND
P.O. Box 4059
Boulder, CO 80306

LONE PEAK
3474 South 2300 East
Salt Lake City, Utah 84109

MADDEN USA
2400 Central Avenue
Dept. MB4
Boulder, CO 80301

ROBERT BECKMAN DESIGNS (formerly Needle Works)
617 North Black
Bozeman, MT 59715
(406) 586-7291

NOTE: This is not intended as an inclusive list of all pannier manufacturers, but, instead, as help in beginning the process of searching for the right saddlebags for your biking style and budget. As suggested in the text, any bike magazine will contain advertisements for additional companies.

The following are two of the rack companies mentioned in the text; again, there are several other brands available through bike shops and catalogues.

BLACKBURN
75 Cristich Lane
Campbell, CA 95008

BRUCE GORDON RACKS
1070 West 2nd Avenue
Eugene, OR 97402

APPENDIX F: *Federal Land Information*

The information provided in Chapter 8, plus state and local offices, should make it clear which areas are off-limits to mountain-bike travel. For further information contact NORBA (address in Appendix C), or write to the following offices:
Bureau of Land Management (BLM)
U.S. Department of the Interior
18th and "C" Streets, N.W.
Room 1013
Washington, DC 20240

National Forests and Wilderness Areas
Forest Service
U.S. Department of Agriculture
12th and Independence Streets, S.W.
P.O. Box 2417
Washington, DC 20013

National Parks and Related Areas
National Park Service
U.S. Department of the Interior
18th and "C" Streets, N.W.
Room 1013
Washington, DC 20240

APPENDIX G: *Touring Companies*

A complete list of bicycle touring companies would require many pages; you
will find names and addresses in the back pages of most cycling magazines. The
following are the four companies with which I've toured.

BACKCOUNTRY BICYCLE TOURS
P.O. Box 4029
Bozeman, MT 59715
(406) 586-3556

BACKROADS BICYCLE TOURING
P.O. Box 1626
San Leandro, CA 94577
(415) 895-1783

RIM TOURS
94 West 1st North
Moab, UT 84532
(801) 259-5223

THE ROAD LESS TRAVELED
P.O. Box 39
West Yellowstone, MT 59758

APPENDIX H: *Miscellaneous Cycle Products*

byKart
P.O. Box 8373
Fountain Valley, CA 92708

CycleTote (trailer)
135 East 4th Street
Loveland, CO 80537
(303) 667-1720

Kroop's Goggles, Inc.
9865-E North Washington Blvd.
Laurel, Maryland 20707
(301) 498-5848

Paul's Cycle Sacs
105 Bennett Avenue
33A
New York, NY 10033
(800) 334-6932
(212) 795-3421 (in-state)

Roly Pearson (Roly caps)
730 West 400 North
Salt Lake City, Utah 84116
(801) 539-8475

APPENDIX I: *Touring Checklist*

Remember that the lengthy list that follows is what I pack on my longest tours. As suggested many times in the text, you will want to personalize your gear to fit your particular requirements.

Clothing

T-shirts (3)	long pants	riding shoes
long-sleeved shirt	gym shorts	camp moccasins
riding shorts (2)	insulated underwear	bandanas (2)
belt	leggings	riding gloves
undershorts (3)	socks (3 pairs)	riding cap

Foul and Cold-Weather Gear

boots	rainsuit	stocking cap
rain boots	goggles	jacket
gaiters	gloves (2 pairs)	vest
rain chaps	overmitts	
poncho	face mask	

Personal

towel	toothbrush case	shampoo
washcloth	toothpaste	waterless hand cleaner
soap	comb	nailbrush
soapdish	toilet paper (partial roll)	fingernail clipper
toothbrush	deodorant	

Shelter and Bedding

tent
sleeping bag
ground pad

Bike Parts

fenders	kickstand	handlebar bag
mirror	riding flag	seat bag
water bottles	toeclips/straps	toe covers (winter tours)
reflectors	racks	rack straps
air pump	saddlebags	

Spare Parts and Tools

tire	spokes (5)	cone wrenches
tube	bearings	chain rivet tool
oil	rack mounting bolts (2)	spoke nipple wrench
grease	6″ crescent wrench	freewheel tool
air gauge	screwdriver	pocket vise
brake cable/gear cable	channel locks	cotterless crank removal tool
brake pad (2)	tire levers (2)	
chain links (3)	allen wrenches	

Miscellaneous

pocket knife
sunglasses/case
flashlight/batteries
camera/film
rope
ripstop repair tape
matches

notebook
book
pen
safety pins
sewing kit
cup
utensil set

can opener
pants clips (2)
map
compass
candle lantern
candles

Medical

sunshade
aspirin (20)
snakebite kit
Desitin
Band-aids (10)
butterfly closure bandages (6)
gauze compress pads (6)
gauze (1 roll)
ace bandages (2)
Benadryl
insect repellent
water purification tablets (or filter-system water purifier, for backcountry rides)
moleskin/2nd skin

Index